KINGSNORTH
AIRSHIP
STATION

US

0

KINGSNORTH AIRSHIP STATION

IN DEFENCE OF THE NATION

TINA BILBÉ

I dedicate this book to my grandfather, whom I never met; my parents, for giving me a love of history; and to my son, Edward, who encouraged me to write this book.

Cover illustrations: Front: NS4 at Kingsnorth, 1918. (Fleet Air Arm Museum A/SHIP 115); Back: C★3 at Kingsnorth, 1918. (Fleet Air Arm Museum E 04635/0001)

First published 2013

The History Press
The Mill, Brimscombe Port
Stroud, Gloucestershire, GL5 2QG
www.thehistorypress.co.uk

British Library Cataloguing in Publication Data.
A catalogue record for this book is available from the British Library.

ISBN 978 0 7524 9153 0

Typesetting and origination by The History Press
Printed in Great Britain

CONTENTS

ACKNOWLEDGEMENTS

This book would never have reached publication without the help of numerous people and I would like to thank: Barbara Gilbert and her colleagues at the Fleet Air Arm Museum for putting me on the right path at the start of my quest, and assisting in finding suitable photographs; the members of all the forums and websites who responded to my barrage of questions and pointed me in the right direction; the nameless dedicated staff at the National Archives who have customer care down to a fine art; Alison Cable and her colleagues at the Medway Archives; Christine McMorris at The History Press, for supporting my proposal for publication; Andrew Dennis and his colleagues at the RAF Museum for enthusiastically hunting out information to continue my enlightenment; all the people whose relatives were at Kingsnorth who have provided information and images for use in this book, including Julie Wantling of Eon, whose grandfather helped build the airship station and whose father helped demolish it; Parveen Sadhi and her colleagues at the Imperial War Museum, for rushing through the final illustrations just in time; and last but not least my husband Graham, who not only ensured I was fed and supplied with endless cups of tea while I worked, but also photographed documents at archives for transcription later and proofread the copy before I sent it off to the publisher.

INTRODUCTION

My father's father died long before I was born. I knew only a little about him from my father's memories, photographs and a few artefacts. As I began researching his life for a family history project, I discovered that much of what my father remembered being told was incorrect. His wartime had not been spent in the Royal Flying Corps, flying observation balloons. Instead he had been in the Royal Naval Air Service, employed as a hydrogen worker at Kingsnorth Airship Station.

This led to more questions. Where was this station? What did a hydrogen worker do? Who was he working with? I started looking for a book or a website that would answer these questions and quickly realised that to find the information I wanted, I would have to search in a lot of places. Not surprisingly, one piece of information led on to a new avenue of research. I joined forums and asked questions, and I am grateful to the many enthusiasts who got back to me with suggestions of where to find information that would help me in my quest. I borrowed and bought books on airships and their role in the First World War. I visited the Fleet Air Arm Museum, the National Archives, the Medway Archives, the Imperial War Museum, the Museum of English Rural Life and the RAF Museum at Hendon.

As I pieced together information from this wide array of sources, I realised that others might be interested in the document I was creating. I began noting my sources so others could track down the raw information, the inclusion of which, though fascinating, would have made this a multi-volume tome.

No doubt as soon as this is published, someone will point out another source of information of which I was unaware, and I will discover more things that I should have included. There will be the odd error, misinterpretation and omission, possibly more than most, as I started from a point of knowing practically nothing. If you find anything amiss, I ask not only your forgiveness but that you take the time to contact me and put me right, quoting your source, in case a second edition is ever called for.

Tina Bilbé
19 April 2013

1

THE SITE

There are two places named Kingsnorth in Kent, one near Ashford and one on the Hoo Peninsula. It was at the second, Kingsnorth Farm on the north bank of the Medway estuary, conveniently close to Gravesend and Chatham, that the Royal Navy chose to build its air station. The military uses for flight, both in terms of airships and aeroplanes, were only just being recognised in the early 1900s, as airships were being developed in continental Europe and the Wright Brothers pioneered aeroplanes in the USA. Airships, with their longer range and greater carrying capacity, looked to be the more promising form of air travel, and aeroplanes, though faster and more manoeuvrable, were seen to have more limited use initially. Craft both heavier and lighter than air were experimented with in the area during the Great War. Had the airships not come to Kingsnorth, it would probably have changed as little over the last hundred years as it had in the century before.

TOPOGRAPHY

Kingsnorth is on the southern shore of the Hoo Peninsula, an area of land stretching between the River Thames to the north and the Medway to the south. 'Hoo' in fact means a spit of land. This low, flat, marshy ground on the north-east Kent coast is bisected by the A228, known locally as Ratcliffe Highway. The area is still dominated by agriculture, in contrast to the urban sprawl of Strood, Rochester, Chatham Naval Dockyard and Gillingham to the south and west.

GEOLOGY

Much of the underlying ground at Kingsnorth consists of sandy silt overlying clay, with an area of gravel to the north-west of the site. The southern area of the site is shown on old maps as Hoo Marsh. Boreholes sunk in 1997 and 1999 revealed a complex sequence of sedimentary deposits laid down over the last 100,000 years.

ARCHAEOLOGY

This low-lying area was subject to flooding so there was never any substantial settlement. A Neolithic flint arrowhead and Beaker pottery indicates that hunting groups passed through and there is evidence of summer grazing and salt-working in the Bronze Age, but these suggest only seasonal use of the area. There are signs of more sustained agriculture during the time of the Roman occupation, with evidence of pottery production and drainage ditches having been cut.

HISTORY

The Hundred of Hoo was owned by Harold Godwinson when he marched to defend his newly acquired kingdom in 1066. William the Conqueror gave Hoo to his half-brother Odo, Bishop of Bayeux, and the Domesday survey gives Beluncle as a manor in this parish, though Kingsnorth and other nearby farms are not mentioned. From the thirteenth century onwards, areas for farming were being enclosed by walls to prevent flooding, but these would have required constant repairs.

In the late seventeenth and early eighteenth centuries, Beluncle Manor was owned by the Cobham family. Richard Webb bought it in 1788, and by 1861 Beluncle and its surrounding farms were owned by William Miskin. On 1 December 1860, Charles Dickens published the first instalment of *Great Expectations* in the weekly periodical *All The Year Round*. The bleak landscape of the Hoo Peninsula is described so vividly that literary historians have been arguing for many years about the exact location of the graveyard where Pip met the convict Magwitch.

EARLY TWENTIETH-CENTURY KINGSNORTH

Between the census of 1851 and that of 1911, Kingsnorth Farm, Barton's Farm and their accompanying cottages were home to an ever-changing array of farm labourers, shepherds, waggoners and carters, along with their wives and children. Beluncle, on higher ground nearer Hoo, is where the farmer Walter Miskin lived.

In 1903 Walter, Arthur and Frank Miskin were in arbitration, regarding the Admiralty's purchase of land for the Chattenden Naval Tramway, and in 1906 Kingsnorth Farm was purchased by the Admiralty so they could use the marshy shoreline for a torpedo range. The farm buildings and arable and grazing land were leased back to Walter Miskin.

Old Beluncle House was destroyed by fire in 1905 and replaced by a modern brick farmhouse. Miskin's only son died in 1908 and around that time he and his wife moved to White Hall Farm, North Street, Hoo. By 1911 Beluncle was occupied by a farmer named James Robinson. At Kingsnorth

A contemporary picture of the area in 1917 from a copy of *Flighty*, RAF Museum, Hendon.

Farm were waggoner Stephen Pope and his wife and three young children. Sparrow Castle housed a shepherd and a farm labourer, both married with children, and three of these men's older sons were working for the government as general labourers (possibly at the munitions depot at Lodge Hill).

A local man, writing about the farm in 1917, remembered that the farm had hedges to create neat fields where flocks of sheep and herds of cattle grazed. Ditches criss-crossed the site in all directions, draining the land. The flowing water in these ditches provided ideal conditions for watercress, and eels were plentiful here. There were several rabbit warrens, wild duck and other game frequented the marshes and the area was a favourite shooting ground for Mr Miskin and his friends. The reed beds in Damhead Fleet were regularly cut for thatching and other uses during the winter months. Arable crops such as swedes were also grown on the farm, the last crop being a field of radishes for seed. The farm workers in the main farmhouse and those in Sparrow Castle had gardens full of produce beside their dwellings. Away from the marshes, cereals, vegetables and fruit were grown.

THE COMING OF THE AIRSHIPS

There are a number of factors to be considered when selecting a site for an airship station: the higher the airships are above sea level, the less lift they have so the less weight they can carry; obstructions such as hills or high buildings in the vicinity must be avoided; and meteorological conditions are very important, as places which are regularly affected by thunderstorms or gusty wind conditions are unsuitable when ships have to be manhandled into their sheds.

When the Royal Navy's director of works at Chatham went to Kingsnorth Farm in the late summer of 1912 during his search for a suitable site to place an airship shed, the flat agricultural landscape at this location seemed ideal for the purpose. It was near to sea level, with prevailing winds north-east and south-west, and the land was already owned by the Admiralty, though leased to the local farmer for grazing, and so by the middle of October they were negotiating to buy back the lease, which still had a couple of years to run, and marking out the ground for the first airship shed. The shed needed to be positioned in line with the prevailing winds to minimise the risk of an airship being caught in a crosswind while being towed into or out of the shed, which could cause considerable damage to the ship.

In January 1913, estimates were made for the cost of building two airship sheds but by February the Admiralty decided the sheds needed to be larger and new estimates had to be drawn up. The cost rose from £52,000 to £63,500. Add to this the £2,504 17s paid to Mr Miskin the farmer for the early surrender of his lease and you can see that this was already a very expensive undertaking. Part of the deal with Miskin was that he would become an Admiralty tenant and pay rent on the grazing and farm buildings until June 1913, at which time the Admiralty had the right to demolish the buildings. Commander Masterman filed a report pointing out that facilities for repairing and refitting the airships would be needed, and that this would not only involve space for the work but also accommodation for the people undertaking the work. He informed the Admiralty of a particular difficulty regarding the maintenance workforce: that the work of sewing envelopes at the Royal Aircraft Factory was principally done by female labour and that the job needed six months' training. He proposed bringing four women in from Farnborough to do this work.

On 20 March 1913, Admiral R. Poore, Commander-in-Chief, the Nore (the Nore is a sandbank at the mouth of the Thames Estuary and gives its name to the navy command responsible for the Thames and Medway areas of the North Sea), wrote to the Admiralty with concerns about the suitability of Kingsnorth as an airship station. The reasons he gave were mainly financial. He knew, from the setting-up of Eastchurch, that the cost of providing accommodation and utilities for a station with some 200 officers and men would be 'heavy'. To these costs would be added those of constructing a road over the marshes and a pier over the mudflats to facilitate access to the site. Secondly, he wrote, 'The position amongst the marshes will probably be unhealthy.' The fact that the buildings in this area were all occupied by agricultural labourers, with the farmers employing them living on higher ground, indicates that this was not an unreasonable assumption. Admiral Poore's suggestion was that the airship station should be sited near the railway, close to Port Victoria. Had his concerns been delivered earlier the site might have been changed, but it appears likely that the acquisition of the site and plans for the sheds were already too advanced for a change of location.

The navy was aware that the marshes throughout the Hoo Peninsula were a breeding ground for mosquitoes and that outbreaks of malaria had been common since Roman times, though less so in the early 1900s. To reduce the chance of another serious outbreak in military establishments, it was decided to avoid sending personnel who had suffered from malaria in the past to serve on the peninsula.

Work on the first airship shed began in April. It took a month to prepare the ground and put in the concrete base before Messrs Hill and Smith Ltd, Constructional Engineers of Brierley Hill, Staffordshire, could begin erection of the steel-framed, iron-clad shed. There were still fifty men working on this shed when the *Chatham News* ran an article about the works at Kingsnorth in August.

Once it had been decided that the naval airship development and production work would be carried on at Kingsnorth, speed of construction became an issue. At the beginning of July 1913, Messrs Vickers Ltd, a leading firm of airship-builders, were given the task of erecting a second shed within three months and, to hurry the job along, they obtained permission to import a prefabricated shed from Germany. This shed, made by Dalacombe, Marechal & Hervieu Ltd was longer than most they produced and the roof was probably clad in corrugated iron for maximum protection from the weather. Although the design was quite complex, the buildings were easy to erect (the company claimed that forty men could erect one in just ten hours) and the speed of erection is certainly why they got the contract.

The purchase of a German-built shed prompted Mr Hunt, the MP for Ludlow, to ask questions about the Admiralty's tendering process. He argued that the work should have benefited British carpenters, many of whom were unemployed at this time. The fact that the contract specified that all the workmen involved in preparing the site and erecting the shed must be British nationals was offered as reassurance that British workmen would benefit from the Admiralty contract.

Work started later in July. The piling for the wooden shed was sub-contracted to Messrs West Bros of Rochester. The imported shed consisted of not only the woodwork but all the metalwork that would be needed for erection, right down to nuts, bolts and screws, and required some 300 railway wagonloads to transport it from Cory's Wharf, Rochester, to Beluncle

Halt, the nearest railway siding to the Kingsnorth site. So much material was required that the siding had to be extended. Transport from Beluncle to the construction site must have been a massive operation, employing considerable amounts of labour.

The design was very clever. The A-frame trestles were erected first at 12ft 6in centres. Each one was fitted with a worm-driven winch for raising (or lowering) the roof. The central portion of the roof trusses was assembled on the ground, including purlins, rafters and canvas covering (or corrugated metal sheeting if in exposed locations), and was then raised high enough to fit the spandrels at either end. The complete roof section was raised by winches and locked in place with automatic catches. The trestles were braced together with wire ropes and the complete shed was then clad. Corrugated iron may have been used to clad the roof; contemporary photographs clearly show wooden sides on this shed.

A large amount of scaffolding was required in order to erect the shed, and sometime during the last three months of 1913 a fatal accident occurred, in which two of the workmen on the site died: John Henry Worker, an experienced scaffolder from St Pancras, aged 55, and Thomas Timms, who was 52 and had a wife and five children, two of whom were still dependent. Timms's widow and children received £291 4s compensation from Vickers. The bodies of both men were returned to London for burial at the cost of £12 10s each. Vickers paid for the funerals and then deducted the funeral expenses from the compensation owed to each family under the Workmen's Act. Timms's widow took Vickers to court and won back the funeral expenses in January the following year. The *Chatham News* reported on the court case. The local undertaker felt so strongly about the way his services had been portrayed that he wrote to the paper to ensure his reputation was not damaged by the case.

Despite the use of a prefabricated shed, it appears to have taken about a year from preparing the ground to the wooden shed being completed and fitted out ready for use.

Contractors employed by the navy were given strict instructions regarding their workforce. They were all to be bona fide British subjects, they had to be suitably housed and there were also clear guidelines on fair wages. Some of the contractors arranged accommodation for their workers in Bell Lane, Hoo St Werburg. Vickers, in addition to constructing the wooden airship shed, were given the job of erecting the silicol plant for hydrogen production and built on-site accommodation for their workers, which later housed naval personnel until suitable bunkhouses were completed.

The hydrogen-generating station, gas tanks and fuel tanks were all situated at the heart of the site, rather than on the far side of the airship sheds, as modern health-and-safety regulations would dictate had they been building

The metal shed on the left with the wooden one beside it under construction in April 1914. To give you an idea of the scale, the dark area between the sheds in front of the triangular structure is a man leading a horse and cart. (Fleet Air Arm Museum, A/STN 0326)

An early aerial photo. The metal airship shed can just be seen in the top left of the picture. The open space in the centre was soon to be filled with buildings and gas tanks to hold the large quantities of hydrogen needed as production of airships increased. (From a photo album donated to the Fleet Air Arm Museum B0412 F/0044)

the station today. The danger of explosion should the purity of the hydrogen be compromised was considerable.

In order to plan the accommodation needed for incoming personnel, Commander Masterman began drawing up reports on what work would be undertaken and estimates of the number of staff required to carry out these duties. Between March and October 1913, the list of staff needed for the smooth running of the station grew, increasing the requirements for accommodation of not only naval personnel but a considerable number of permanent civilian workers.

Accommodation for naval personnel was less than ideal, and as the year progressed barrack huts for the 120 single men who would be arriving in May the following year to work on the airships were needed as urgently as sheds for airships. On 8 November 1913, page 7 of the *Chatham News* carried a column about this, stating that the Admiralty was asking both the District and Parish Councils to assist them in finding accommodation for eighty married men and their families. There were not enough existing cottages available in the area and builders were having difficulty raising the money to build more to house the Admiralty staff because a change in government policy might empty them just as suddenly as the requirement had arisen.

By the end of May, Commander Masterman had started submitting lists of equipment that would be required for the airship workshops dealing with maintenance of the ballonet envelopes, woodwork relating to the hull (car, stabilising planes and so on), engines and auxiliary machinery, and rigging. The following month he resubmitted his list of civilian repair staff for airship bases and added to it draughtsmen, an instrument-maker, a photographer and a pensioner to serve as chief armourer. Commander Masterman concluded, 'I consider the early training of the naval repair staff fully as important as the training of the airship crews & handling parties, since the one is useless without the other.'

Chatham's Director of Works, John H. Oakley, and the Superintending Civil Engineer, John W. Stone, soon realised that they needed more land for the growing airship station. They had already approached Mr Miskin in December 1912 and he passed the matter on to his solicitor for advice.

On 24 July 1913, Oakley and Stone submitted a request to the Admiralty for the purchase of an additional 81½ acres. The Admiralty surveyor, another Mr Oakley, had valued the land at £30 an acre, as only 19 of the 81½ acres was arable land (the rest being marsh). However Mr Miskin's solicitors estimated that the land was worth over £104 an acre, on the grounds of its connection to Admiralty works and property adjoining. Proximity to the railway would also have increased its value. The Admiralty decided that a compulsory purchase order would be expensive and that arbitration might uphold a higher

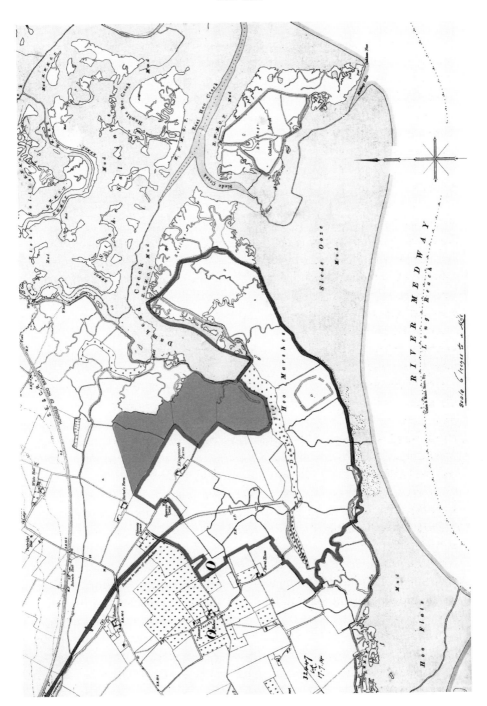

The land originally bought by the Admiralty is surrounded by a thick outline and the land they wished to purchase to extend the station shaded in grey. The proposed railway extension from Beluncle Halt can be seen coming in from the top left corner of the map. (Medway Archives SRDC/982/8)

valuation on the land, so they gave permission for an initial offer of £2,445 to be made and, should that offer be rejected, a second offer of £4,250 be made. The Admiralty was keen to take possession by Christmas 1913 but Miskin was in no hurry to sell his land at Barton's Farm and held out for a higher price. He also refused the suggestion that he lease the land to the Admiralty. By February 1914, the Admiralty were again considering compulsory purchase but eventually terms were agreed with Miskin's solicitors and there followed an extended correspondence between April and September 1914 to complete the purchase.

While negotiations were being undertaken for the land, plans for improving facilities at the site were being proposed. A folder of correspondence between Commander Masterman RN, Farnborough, the officer in charge of the Naval Airship Wing, and H.E. Oakley, the Superintending Civil Engineer at Chatham Dockyard (this appears to be a third Oakley who had taken over from John W. Stone) gives detailed information regarding what was being built and how much it was costing.

The estimate for works, dated 2 January 1914, includes ground-clearance and the construction of clearing ditches, the building of new roads, a pier and a light railway, the erection of a boiler house, an electric light and power station, a hydrogen generating station, putting in a water supply for drinking and to the electric and hydrogen generating stations, a coal store, petrol store, oil store, engineers' workshop, garage, blacksmith's forge, first-aid room, an office and an explosives store. Also required were one steel shed (Hill and Smith) with tinted glass windows, trenches for rails and sleepers, concrete under doorways, electric cable pits and pipes and hydrogen trenches, one timber shed (Vickers), plus an extra charge for doors and housing accommodation (presumably for the doors to slide in), handling arrangements for airships (for example, mooring rings) and a wireless station. Separate quarters and mess arrangements were required for men, officers and petty officers, and a cookhouse, meat store and latrines also needed to be built. There were fire-prevention arrangements for the boiler house and trenches for steam heating.

The cost was around £130,000. Mr W. Harbrow, J.C. Whettam and a builder who simply used the initials J.W.G. were three of the building firms who benefited from this expansion. Many of the buildings at Kingsnorth used the same basic architectural plans as would have been used for erecting buildings overseas. They were colonial-style, single-storey buildings constructed mainly of wood and galvanised iron, which were very quick and easy to put up in most environments. If the records of Messenger & Co. Ltd, another of the contractors working on the site a few months later, are a good representation of the amount of work involved in building accommodation for the men, then a hut housing sixteen men in hammocks cost just over £166 and took

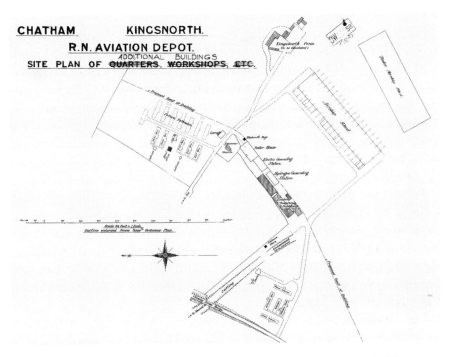

Building plans for increasing the accommodation and facilities. The main farm buildings were still standing to the east of the airship sheds when this plan was drawn up. (National Archives AIR 1/408/15/236/2)

four men about six weeks to build from start to finish. Building work was seriously hampered by the muddy conditions.

The following year, 1915, more buildings were required to cater for the growing needs of the station. These included a laundry as well as rubber and dope laboratories.

The station required not only buildings and personnel but fixtures and furnishings. Requisition orders for equipment were also underway: stoves for cooking and heating the galvanised-iron huts, fire extinguishers and medical supplies were added to those for sewing machines and tools for the production and maintenance of the airships.

Another necessity was rapid communication, and arrangements were made to switch the telephone line known as Chatham 1 to Kingsnorth, with the proviso that it could be quickly reconnected to Chatham when the commander-in-chief at the Nore required it.

Commander Usborne was appointed to the command of Kingsnorth Airship Station in April 1914.

During May and June personnel began to arrive at Kingsnorth and the newly appointed Commander Usborne was concerned that off-duty men would spend time in Hoo or Rochester. He described Hoo as, 'a particularly undesirable village, full of public houses of the low agricultural type'. And on these grounds, towards the end of June, he requested permission for a 'wet canteen' on site so the consumption of alcohol would be under his control. He proposed providing games and indoor recreation facilities and had future plans for garden allotments and so on, 'so there is no reason why the place should not become a happy, self contained, colony'. F.R. Scarlett, the inspecting Captain of Aircraft based at Sheerness, had no such illusions. He stated his opinion that 'its provision would not prevent liberty men visiting Hoo and Rochester'. Nevertheless, Commander Usborne got his wet canteen.

As the station developed, a large number of new staff and builders started to arrive. As a consequence, orders were given to sentries guarding the airship sheds regarding increased security. The lack of office accommodation was also causing problems and a request for furniture that could be used in the officers' mess as an interim measure was made.

THE FORMATION OF THE RNAS

In the first decade of the 1900s, both the army and the Royal Navy had been developing aerial capabilities. In 1912, the Committee of Imperial Defence decided to amalgamate the Army Air Battalion and the Air Wing of the Navy to form the Royal Flying Corps, consisting of two wings. The naval wing was under the command of Commander C.R. Sampson but in overall control was Director David Henderson, who had been Director of Military Intelligence for a decade.

The navy was unhappy about its air support being under the control of the Royal Flying Corps, which they perceived as being controlled by the army, so on 23 June 1914 the navy gained permission to break away and formed the Royal Naval Air Service. By mutual consent all airships were transferred to the RNAS. Admiralty papers in the National Archives indicate that the Astra-Torres airship was already at Kingsnorth and official transfer of the Parseval, two newly completed airships, experimental work and accompanying personnel from Farnborough took place on 27 July. One source says that Kingsnorth Airship Station was finished by June 1914 and another that it was still under construction at the time of the move. The decision to relocate the development programme was almost certainly the factor which necessitated further building work. From the documents, it appears that the Royal Navy were already planning for the move about six months before the formation of the RNAS was announced. Buildings for storage and manufacture, along with experimental laboratories and a large power house, were added to the original station. The assassination of Archduke Franz Ferdinand on 28 June 1914 was the incident that started the war but it is clear that tensions had been growing for some time and war came as no surprise to the British Armed Forces.

DURING THE FIRST WORLD WAR

When Britain joined the war on 4 August 1914, Wing Commander Usborne, commanding officer at Kingsnorth, reported on the personnel at the station. Including himself there were nine officers, seventy-seven Air Service ratings, an airship 'handling party' of forty-eight boys and two petty officers on loan from a nearby depot, a military guard of two officers, and sixty-two NCOs and men, plus one officer and twenty-nine men building a blockhouse, which was some distance away from the main complex of buildings as it is not on the 1916 site plan. Accommodation was not ideal. Military personnel were accommodated in tents and the handling party were in the former Vickers workmen's buildings.

A telephone was installed in the petty officers' cabin, which was situated between two living rooms. Unfortunately it was difficult to hear when the telephone rang and a request was sent off for an extension bell on 9 November.

Once orders for building work had been sent out, tenders were invited for the supply of tools. Tenders were accepted and orders placed towards the end of September for a coppersmith's forge, grindstones for sharpening tools, a hacksawing machine, a drilling machine and a 20in pillar drill.

By 17 October, foundations had been laid for a cooling tower and fuel oil-storage tanks. A machinery house was also under construction, with the intention of housing an oil-driven electricity generating plant for the station by the end of January 1915.

At the beginning of November, the new silicol plant, which was to supply hydrogen for the airships, was being tested. The geology was causing problems, with the water supply carrying large quantities of sand and grit into the machinery. To get around this, it was proposed to add a large tank into the water system, which would need to be cleared of sediment every two hours.

The coal stores at Kingsnorth were used to supply ships as well as for hydrogen production.

On 26 November 1914, HMS *Bulwark*, a 15,000-ton battleship, was moored at buoy no. 17 at Keyhole Reach on the River Medway, taking on coal from Kingsnorth. At 7.50 a.m., as the crew were having breakfast, an explosion ripped the ship apart. Debris from the explosion fell up to 4 miles away. Of the 810 crew on board, only nine survived and they were all badly wounded.

The local papers immediately suspected sabotage. Another ship had coal loaded by the same group of workmen and disappeared soon after, so the reporter suspected one of those men was responsible. The subsequent naval court of enquiry (held at the Royal Naval Hospital, Gillingham) found that much of the ammunition for the ship's guns had been stored in the corridors between the eleven magazines, and that either a fault with one of the shells or overheating cordite near a boiler room bulkhead could have started a chain

HMS *Bulwark* around 1900. (Michael Pocock, Maritime Quest website)

reaction which destroyed the ship. The wreckage is still there and is now classified as an official war grave.

During November and December 1914, building work was continuing. An officers' and men's mess, was erected and also accommodation for fourteen men (described as a 'hut' in the contract) was put up by Messenger and Co., a Loughborough-based horticultural builder. The Admiralty stressed that all the workers must be bona fide British subjects and required the firm to provide a list of their workforce. Messenger's foreman was F. Harris and his reports confirm that Admiral Poore's predictions about the difficulties of the site were well founded. There were delays getting the building materials to the site from Sharnal Street Station to Beluncle, and more getting them from Beluncle to the site. The rain in early December softened the ground so they were wading about in soft clay and the manager at head office was frequently writing to ask why things were taking so long.

On 29 December, Foreman Harris reported to head office that there had been a serious gale that had done a lot of damage. The top of one of the airship sheds had been blown off and glass was blown out of the windows of many of the huts.

Mr Oakley, the supervising civil engineer, must have been reasonably satisfied with the work as he used Messenger and Co. again in 1915 to build a second motor garage. The subcontractors used by the firm seemed less impressed with them, as there is correspondence in Messenger's files of firms chasing them for payment.

The overall site foreman, Mr Ferrett, put contractors in touch with John Blackman, a local carter from Pearce's Farm, 5 Bell Lane, Hoo. He was apparently the only local man with a cart available to transport goods from Beluncle Halt to the airship site. (Charlie Mills, the local carrier, was probably only set up to carry items by road and his wagon would have been unsuitable for the boggy conditions at Kingsnorth.) The builders at Kingsnorth needed to get supplies of building materials quickly and considered that their job should be Mr Blackman's top priority. Unfortunately for them, John Blackman found the two-mile trip from the farm broke up his day so he was unable to undertake other tasks, and he was more interested in ensuring the needs of his regular employers were met. This was the cause of considerable friction during both building jobs undertaken by Messenger and Co.

Commander Usborne's expertise in developmental work, gained with Vickers in Barrow, may have been one of the factors that led Commander Masterman to choose Kingsnorth as the station to undertake development of non-rigid airships. Once it was confirmed that Kingsnorth was to undertake this experimental work for developing the Admiralty's airship capability, even more facilities were needed for the growing workforce. The temporary buildings that had been put up to house the Vickers workforce were replaced by a couple of long two-storey brick buildings in 1915.

In March 1915, the remaining design staff and equipment arrived from Farnborough. The need for laboratory space for rubber and dope testing were

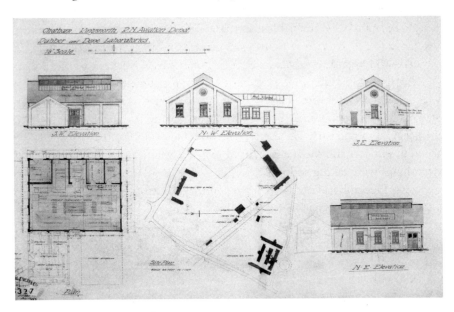

Plans for the rubber and dope laboratory dated August 1915. (Fleet Air Arm Museum 2011/127/0016)

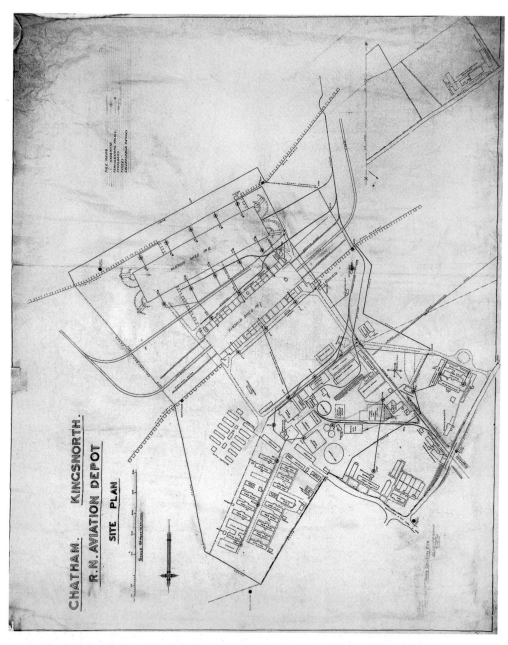

Site plan, dating from about 1917, showing how much the site had changed in the course of a year. Compare it to the earlier plan and aerial photograph. The timber shed has been extended. (Fleet Air Arm Museum 2011/127/0001)

Taken in 1917, this shows the site from the same angle as the plan above. The railway track curves round past the hydrogen production plant and runs in front of the airship sheds. (Fleet Air Arm Museum 1978/104/0001)

identified and plans were drawn up by J.C. Whettam during the second half of the year.

Around this time, a training school was opened at the station to train both pilots and ground crew, who were needed in increasing numbers to operate the ever-expanding fleet of airships. By the end of 1915, thirty-six trainee pilots had passed out as fully-fledged airship captains, 139 riggers and numerous other maintenance and handling ratings had also completed their training.

At the end of 1916, training was moved to RNAS Cranwell so that Kingsnorth could concentrate on assembly, repair and design.

In January 1917, the silicol plant, which had been supplying hydrogen for the airships, was supplemented by a water gas plant. By the end of July, the wooden airship shed had been extended to accommodate the larger airships being designed and built on the station, and in September new bottle-filling sheds were proposed to a standard design that would be used at a number of other stations as well.

The dimensions of the first airship shed were 555ft (length) by 109ft (width) by 100ft (height). This was the Hill and Smith steel shed to the north. The second shed was 700ft long by 150ft wide by 98ft high. This was the German timber shed erected by Vickers, with its distinctive curved roof.

In November 1918, immediately after the signing of the Armistice, suggestions were made regarding the future of the Airship Service within the newly formed Royal Air Force. A report was drafted which pointed out the problems, for both the Royal Navy and the RAF, with the set-up in place at the time, and proposals for putting both airships and airship personnel under the remit of the Royal Navy. This fourteen-page document carefully detailed the current situation and proposals for the future, including stations with hydrogen plants in operation. Kingsnorth was top of the list, with a new electrolytic plant under construction, which, with other facilities, led to a recommendation that the plant-construction programme be completed and that Kingsnorth undertake various pieces of construction work on non-rigid airships. Had these proposals been accepted, Kingsnorth might have continued to flourish as a naval airship dockyard, but the RAF decided to concentrate on rigid airships and Kingsnorth became a backwater.

In 1919, the RAF were looking for a suitable site to continue experimenting with kite balloons and Kingsnorth was put forward as ideal, given that all the necessary infrastructure was already in place there. The Admiralty were using the airship sheds for storing mines but were asked to remove them to make way for the equipment being cleared from the stores at Earls Court, which were being decommissioned between August and October. Although the transfer was initially agreed, it soon became apparent that the Admiralty were having problems finding a suitable space to move the mines into and the whole plan seems to have fallen through.

TRANSPORT

By Sea

Kingsnorth workers did not all live within easy distance of the airship base and a small paddle steamer, PS *Audrey*, and its captain were commandeered for use by the navy to ferry workers to and from Chatham.

Built by Armstrong, Whitworth and Co. in 1897, the *Audrey* spent the first twelve years of her life ferrying up and down the Tyne before leaving the North-East for Cork, where she spent another five years. She was bought by Captain Sidney Shippick in 1914 and used for excursions on the south coast, around the Bournemouth, Swanage and Poole areas, until she was taken over by the Admiralty. *Audrey* was not released from Admiralty service until 1922. Captain Shippick reacquired her on behalf of the New Medway Steam Packet Co., where he had just become managing director.

She was reconditioned and employed on a variety of duties including excursions to Herne Bay and over to Southend, and river cruises. Shippick and *Audrey* transformed the business, laying the foundations for a company that survives to this day. The *Audrey* ended her service and was withdrawn at the end of the 1929 season, sold to T.W. Ward's yard at Grays for £500 and broken for scrap, a sad end for the old lady.

PS *Audrey* in the 1920s. The aft deck was at least twice the area of the one at the bow. (Ian Boyle/Simplon Postcards)

By Rail

The Chattenden Naval Tramways order of 1901 authorised the construction of a standard-gauge railway from Lodge Hill down to the pier to the south of Kingsnorth Farm on the River Medway. At this time, only the section from the sidings at Sharnal Street to the munitions depot at Lodge Hill was built by the War Department. This line was transferred to the Admiralty on 2 April 1906, the same year the marshes south of Kingsnorth Farm were acquired for a torpedo range. The continuation of the other part of the line linking Lodge Hill to Kingsnorth was not built until the coming of the airship station and the outbreak of the First World War. Abbotts Court Pier and the railway connection opened in 1915, linking the air station to the Hundred of Hoo Railway between Sharnal Street and Lodge Hill, both aided the transit of heavy materials. As the line entered the airbase, it split. One line went off to the hydrogen plant, where it split again into three sidings with a loop. The other line went towards the airship sheds, with another siding serving the stores and boiler house. This line passed to the west of the sheds and terminated just beyond them.

In addition to the standard-gauge line, there was a narrow-gauge (2ft 6in) line which started behind the stores building and ran south. It split, with a siding running off between the airship sheds and the longer stretch of the line crossed the standard gauge on the flat and then went up on to an embankment to cross the Damhead Fleet pools heading down to the pier. There was also a run of 10ft-gauge track that ran through the metal airship shed, extending a little at each end. Traditionally the airships were moved in and out of the

Lord Fisher working at Hilsea Gasworks in the late 1950s. (Industrial Railway Society 10915)

sheds by large teams of ground crew but this broad-gauge track was part of an experiment to move the ships using a powered trolley. (Details of this are in Chapter 2, Research and Production.)

The airship station had its own locomotive, an 0-4-0 saddle tank despatched by Andrew Barclay & Sons Co. Ltd of Kilmarnock on 7 September 1915, No. 1398. It was named *Lord Fisher*, after Admiral John Fisher, 1st Lord Kilverstone. Admiral 'Jacky' Fisher was the First Sea Lord from 1904 to 1910 and a great naval reformer, returning to the position of First Sea Lord at the start of the war in 1914 but resigning on 15 May 1915 after the Gallipoli fiasco. He then moved to the Board of Innovations, where he was responsible for ordering the development of what became the SS-class airship. The Kingsnorth men clearly had a fondness, respect and admiration for this man, which manifested itself in their referring to the engine which carried his name as 'Jacky'.

There was also a narrow-gauge 0-4-0 saddle tank called *Nipper*. This engine, No. 1895, had been built for the Admiralty by W.G. Bagnall in 1909 and was transferred to Kingsnorth from Hoo Ness on 16 May 1916.

After the war, the rail access and pier added greatly to the value of the site when the Admiralty made the decision to dispose of it. The engine *Lord Fisher* was sent to the Royal Aircraft Establishment at Farnborough when the Kingsnorth site was decommissioned. It was then used at a number of MOD and private locations: it was at Camberley Gasworks in 1956 and moved to Hilsea Gasworks and then on to Southampton Gasworks in 1960. It was fully overhauled and worked at the Chapel Tramway, an industrial line near Southampton docks. *Lord Fisher* was withdrawn from service on the closure of the tramway in May 1967. Reinstated briefly, it was the last engine to work on the Longmoor Steam Railway, an old military railway system, and was involved in the clearing-up operations in October 1971 after Columbia Pictures filmed *Young Winston*.

Lord Fisher is still in preservation, was overhauled and has been working on the East Somerset Railway since September 2000. The current owner, Barry Buckfield, had it completely stripped down and overhauled, returning it to service in the autumn of 2012. It is currently at Yeovil.

Less is known of the fate of *Nipper*, other than that it had returned to Hoo Ness by the end of 1918.

By Road

The railways seem to have been used mainly for goods but there were at least three large garages on site in 1917, sheltering several lorries, and references in *Flighty*, the station magazine, suggest that there was some kind of charabanc or bus that was used as the 'liberty boat', taking off-duty men into Strood or Rochester. There was also a Rover touring car (1146) used by officers, which was supposed to be kept for official duties but was purloined for joyriding from time to time, and a Foden steam lorry.

1920–PRESENT

In the years following the First World War, defence cuts became the order of the day. Kingsnorth Airship Station was very important to the local economy, employing large numbers of local civilians in such activities as fabric-working, so it would have been a great blow to them when, in 1920, it was closed and development work was transferred to Cardington in Bedfordshire. Confirmation that the site was to be relinquished was recorded on 25 August 1921.

Flight magazine, published weekly by the Aero Club of the UK, had the following report in the edition dated 2 February 1922:

> **Kingsnorth For Sale** – Following the Government decision to 'scrap the lot', the various airship stations are gradually being entirely evacuated, or the personnel reduced to care and maintenance parties. Among the latest airship stations, although described by the Disposal Board as a Kite Balloon Station, to be advertised for sale, is Kingsnorth, near Chatham. This station comprises about 600 acres, and already has a number of buildings and one large airship shed [sic]. In view of its location, and with the existing facilities of railway connection to Sharnal Street Station on the S.E. & C.R. and its jetty on the Medway, it would appear that Kingsnorth is admirably suited as a terminus for airship services when and if such are started. It therefore appears a somewhat doubtful policy on the part of the Government to offer this site for sale just now, as it could quickly and with but small outlay be got ready for serving as the London 'port' for airship services. The erection of a mooring mast and a few other additions to the existing equipment would be all that was required, the ships, of course, going to a suitable base, such as Pulham, for repairs and overhaul, much as a steamer now goes into dry dock. Kingsnorth would appear to be much more suited for the purpose than is, for instance, Croydon aerodrome, and we would urge upon those in authority to consider the advisability of retaining Kingsnorth for a time at any rate, so that if, as does not seem improbable, airships are to be given a chance, the station is available as a small beginning during the experimental stages. Later, if it be found that the services grow to such an extent as to require other arrangements, the authorities would be no worse off through having retained the station.

In 1922, Messrs Holm & Co. Ltd acquired the Kingsnorth Balloon Stores Depot to accommodate equipment used for pulping timber for the paper and chemical industries. The firm was owned by Alfred Amundsen Holm, a Norwegian wood-pulp merchant who lived in a large house in Putney Park Avenue, London. They also acquired the pier, land fronting on to the Medway and the 'private railway track'. The Disposals Board had indicated that this track, which was part of the Chattenden Naval Tramway, originally authorised in 1901, would enable them to have a rail link to the Southern Railway track at Sharnal Street Station. However, the Admiralty were still using the track to transport munitions and stores to and from their magazine at Lodge Hill, and were not keen to share the track with a company that had no experience in running a railway. Holm & Co. applied for a Light Railway Order in November 1925, which was turned down in February 1926, but an improved application was made and Order No. 476 was granted in November 1926. It was not until the rail connection had been sought that Holm and Co., Ship and Mill Owners registered an entry in Kelly's Directories. A second Light Railway Order, No. 490 of July 1929, transferred the power to run this line from Holm and Co. to the Kingsnorth Light Railway Company, under which title it operated until 1940.

As the Andrew Barclay engine *Lord Fisher* was not sold with the railway line, the Kingsnorth Light Railway obtained and operated a 1921 Kerr Stuart 0-4-0 saddle-tank engine (works no. 4227), which was later transferred to Woolwich Arsenal, and a pair of Hardy petrol locomotives.

The timber-pulping business moved to Cuxton around 1928 and the wooden shed was sold to a local farmer for use as a barn. He reduced the height, using only the top third of the building, which provided commodious accommodation compared to most commercially available prefabricated barns. RNAS Admiralty numbers KBIIIWH stamped on the frame were used to identify the shed and it is now a Grade II listed building.

In about 1928, 323 acres of the site were purchased by Berry Wiggins & Co. Ltd, who by 1930 had started manufacturing bitumen there and in the 1960s built an oil refinery. In the early years they made extensive use of the existing facilities, including the buildings, river pier and internal railway. A dispute between Berry Wiggins and Kingsnorth Light Railway resulted in the oil company constructing their own sidings and connection directly to the Port Victoria Branch at Beluncle Halt, about half a mile away. They replaced the river pier with a much longer jetty in 1937, and in 1940 they abandoned the internal railway. The rails were scrapped for the war effort during the Second World War. By 1964 they had an annual capacity of 190,000 tons and work started on a second jetty, which came into operation in 1967. (There are two aerial photographs taken around 1930 in the English Heritage collection *Britain from Above*.)

By the early 1960s, this area of the Hoo Peninsula was becoming increasingly heavily industrialised. The Central Electricity Generating Board

Kingsnorth Power Station viewed from the river. (Eon)

constructed Kingsnorth Power Station, to the south of the Berry Wiggins site, between 1963 and 1973, one of ten 2,000-megawatt electricity-generating stations built during that period. There were both coal and oil options within the complex and two large jetties in the River Medway for both colliers and oil tankers. Coal-fired generation was the predominant power source after 1978. In addition, there was a back-up gas turbine station.

Although Mr Alfred Holm had sold most of the site, he kept his house, known as The Lodge, and seems to have moved his family there around 1936, which suggests money might have become a little tight. After his death on 5 July 1942, his wife Maud continued to live there until her death on 4 March 1949 and his elderly, unmarried daughters also lived there until they too died. Floey passed away in 1969 and her younger sister Phyllis was still officially living there in 1975 when Mr S.H. Bergman photographed many of the remaining RNAS buildings that were still on the site. She died in 1980 and the house slowly fell into disrepair.

In early 1970, a BBC scout was travelling to Kingsnorth Power Station looking for a suitable location to film an episode of *Doctor Who*, which had just begun its first season in colour with Jon Pertwee in the title role. Before he reached the power station, the location scout came to the Berry Wiggins site and decided to look no further. As a result, millions of viewers saw the Doctor, his companion Liz Shaw and an alternate-reality version of the UNIT members, led by Brigadier Alistair Gordon Lethbridge-Stewart, ducking and diving round the storage tanks and facilities. Keen railway enthusiasts spotted the

Berry Wiggins railway wagons and tanker lorries and so quickly identified the site where hairy green human mutants and the alternative UNIT forces had to be outwitted before the Doctor and Liz could escape back to their own reality!

The Berry Wiggins plant ceased operation in 1977 and was sold to British Petroleum. The timber-framed buildings were abandoned but the two brick store buildings continued to be used, though they were extensively modified. In 1980, the refinery was demolished but the oil-storage and research facilities were retained. At the end of December 1986, John Davis, the member of staff in charge of the development office at BP Aquaseal, was tidying up his office and emptied a number of drawers containing papers that had lain there undisturbed for years. He was surprised to see the dates were 1914–1918 and there were a number of building plans and a blueprint – a wiring diagram for one of the airships. It is finds like this one, which was donated to the Fleet Air Arm Museum in Yeovilton, that have provided such a rich source of material for research. The storage facilities continued to be used by BP as a depot for imported refined oil until 1999.

When BP closed, the northern part of the site became Kingsnorth Industrial Estate. Occupants of this high-security estate are constantly changing as small businesses come and go.

Kingsnorth Power Station was the focus of controversy over Eon's proposals to build another coal-fired generator on the site. In October 2007, five Greenpeace activists climbed one of the chimneys of the coal-fired station to protest about its contribution to climate change. A Climate Camp was set up outside the power station the following year. Plans for a second carbon-capture-ready coal-fired station were put on hold in 2009 at the beginning of the recession and the plans were withdrawn in 2010 due to the economic climate. In March 2012, Eon announced that the current coal-fired units would close in 2013, as they had opted not to adapt them to meet EU emissions targets. This is still an ideal site for power generation and a more environmentally friendly power station may replace the old coal-fired units at some future date. There are proposals for more industrial development in the area.

Comparing the Ordnance Survey Map of 1914 with a modern map or satellite image, you can see how the airship station site has developed into a modern industrial area. Beyond the line of the old airship station, only Chimney Corner and Barton's Farm, now just a yard, have gone, though Burnt House and other buildings north of the station on Jacob's Lane are still there, though possibly extended or rebuilt over the years. Kingsnorth House is relatively new. The orchards are gone, replaced by other crops, but much of the marshland in the west of the site remains a welcome haven for wetland wildlife. The salt marsh island of Oakham, just off Eshcol Road, was turned into a nature reserve and two cottages were converted into the

Kingsnorth Power Station Nature Study Centre in the 1990s. Here thousands of schoolchildren visited each year to learn about the flora, fauna and ecology of the area. The marshlands are used by wildfowl and waders during migration periods and also support nesting avocets. Around 200 species of bird have been recorded here, and there are approximately twenty bird and bat boxes. Sticklebacks and great crested newts compete to thrive and two rare orchids can also be found amongst the silver birch trees.

As well as the top third of the Vickers' airship shed that survives at the nearby farm, stores buildings B and C, situated just north of where the airship sheds used to stand, are still in use as rented space for small start-up companies. At least one other building has survived elsewhere on the industrial-estate site.

By the time you are looking at this book, the skyline of Hoo marshes will have changed again as the power station is decommissioned. Hopefully the nature reserve will find another patron. (Eon)

2

RESEARCH AND PRODUCTION

The officers brought together at Kingsnorth had worked on airships at Barrow and Farnborough. Senior officers had also visited airship-makers in Europe before the war. This experience was very important, as a report in *Flight* magazine during December 1913 points out the difficulties of airship design given the paucity of available information on them at that time. The Kingsnorth team were ideally placed to use their combined expertise to build on this earlier research.

Wing Commander Usborne was noted for his innovative ideas. Towards the end of October 1914, he put forward an idea that would increase the usefulness of airships. This idea had the additional benefit of giving aircrews an alternative to the monotony of sea patrols. While new airship designs were being considered, he suggested that two airships, HMA *No. 3* and HMA *No. 8*, be used for 'aggressive' missions. The idea was that these airships could be towed across the North Sea and then undertake night flights during cloudy weather. They would be equipped with canoes that could be lowered below the clouds, enabling an observer in the canoe to communicate the airship's position and ensure it was correctly manoeuvred over a target. The airship would then be able to attack from a low height by dropping bombs.

The first sea battle of the war was fought in the straits between Germany and Heligoland, a small archipelago in the North Sea that had been under British rule since the Napoleonic wars but was exchanged for African territories in 1890. Like Gibraltar, it had been heavily fortified by the British, and Germany developed it as a submarine base. The main island itself was very difficult to attack and was suggested as a particularly suitable target for a bombing operation by airship.

Towing trials on 2 November 1914 proved successful and by 17 November an observation car for lowering from the airship had been prepared. The experiment with the observation car worked well, but high winds and problems with other airships militated against the idea and it was never implemented.

SUBMARINE OR SEA SCOUT AIRSHIPS

Following increased losses of ships to submarine attacks during October and November 1914, the need for a simply designed and easily produced airship became urgent. The First Sea Lord, Lord Fisher, called together Commander Masterman (commander of the RNAS), Wing Commander Usborne and representatives from Vickers (who had been involved in building the ill-fated *Mayfly*) and Airships Ltd on 28 February. There was no time for extensive experimentation or the elaboration of new designs; speed in production was essential, and speed could not be attained except by the adaptation of existing types and the use of standard parts.

Kingsnorth Station Commander Usborne and Wing Commander Cave-Brown-Cave were in the mess at Farnborough with Mr F.M. Green of the Royal Aircraft Factory when their conversation turned to the new airship requirements and it was here that the initial idea for the 'SS'-class airships was born. The fact that Usborne and Cave-Brown-Cave were involved from the start of the project ensured that the design and production team had a clear idea of what was required. Work commenced on this ship on 22 February 1915. The development of the Eta patch at the Royal Aircraft Factory, Farnborough, in 1912 meant that anything could be attached directly to the gas envelope, subject to weight and aerodynamic forces. This enabled the Kingsnorth team to attach a BE2c aeroplane fuselage beneath the envelope of the Willows *No. 2* gasbag, thereby creating an airship. The main difficulty was in getting the car suitably balanced below the envelope, each time an Eta patch was moved the team had to wait twenty-four hours for the patch to dry before testing whether the new position was an improvement. It was very important that the control-cable tension was right or steering the ship was impossible.

Sea Scout 1 (*SS1*) was officially ready on 6 March 1915 and underwent rigorous testing before it was put into service at Kingsnorth on 18 March. Including testing, it took less than a month to complete. The team was then asked to build more to fill the urgent need for naval air support. Even after it was put into service, two more months of fine-tuning took place before the final design was completed and *SS1* left Kingsnorth to take up patrol duties at Capal near Dover on 7 May. Unfortunately, en route to Dover, the *SS1*, travelling with the wind at nearly 50mph, overshot the landing ground and crashed into some telegraph lines (that is, the rigging between the car and the envelope struck the lines). The broken telegraph wires gave off a shower of sparks. Almost instantly the envelope caught fire below and was very rapidly consumed. The occupants managed to jump clear as the ship hit the wires and fell to the ground, some 15ft or so. They were uninjured except for bruises and scorching. This ended the working life of *SS1* before it had even begun.

SS1 being led out of the shed at Kingsnorth. (Imperial War Museum HU_128831)

Over the next couple of years another forty-eight SS-class airships were built, using *SS1* as a basic pattern. Once the Kingsnorth team had designed and built the first batch of Submarine Scout airships, production began at other stations to meet the high demand. Wormwood Scrubs, Folkestone and Barrow each produced some of the forty-eight Submarine Scouts that were built over the next few years, and most airship stations modified the ships in their charge to suit the local conditions.

Commander Usborne arranged for the envelopes to be made by waterproof-garment manufacturers. The car designed by Armstrong Whitworth was chosen over that of Airships Ltd, and most of them were manufactured by Sage & Co. Ltd of Peterborough, a company that before the war had been exclusively involved in the business of producing shop fittings. Envelopes and cars were transported to Kingsnorth, where they were joined together.

Victor Goddard and Thomas Blenheim Williams provided the Imperial War Museum with vivid descriptions of early airship production. The two hangar floors were covered with airships in various stages of construction, about three or four ships in each hangar. Pilots, as part of their training, constructed the ship in which they would be flying; this must have resulted in a high level of quality control and ensured each pilot knew his ship's construction in the finest detail. Envelopes, cars, rigging and 150ft control wires, rudder planes, flaps and elevators, nose stiffeners, valves, and two ballonets for containing gas were all collected and the pilot then supervised the construction. Ships were being constructed at a rate of about one per week using this method.

MOVING AIRSHIPS INTO AND OUT OF THE SHED USING A MOORING TROLLEY

On 23 November 1915, trials were carried out using a mooring trolley and special trucks originally designed for use with a rigid airship. The trolley was powered by a 60hp engine and ran on 10ft-gauge rails laid through the airship shed and out each end. Parallel to this track ran two standard-gauge tracks, one either side, for the trucks, used to keep the airship in line with the shed and to hold it steady as it passed the windscreens.

For this experiment, the *Delta* envelope was inflated and rigged to a pair of large wooden beams. The envelope was protected from damage on the truck by a pair of pads, one under the envelope and one on top of the trolley. The airship and truck were fastened with a steel cable so that the pads came together. As the trial started, there was a light easterly breeze blowing. It was decided to remove some ballast, which caused the pads to separate. The trolley

Close-up of the central truck and booms from 'Airship Experimental Report 1915' shows the ship well under control. (RAF Museum, Hendon)

A wider view with the protective pads clearly visible at the top of the structure on the forward trolley, 'Airship Experimental Report 1915'. (RAF Museum, Hendon)

started and two minutes later the guys were cast off. Almost immediately the pads swung apart and five minutes later the ship swung round with its nose to the wind. On the return journey the ship rocked considerably, striking the ground with its booms several times. The attachment to the top of the trolley became disconnected and the ship was then controlled by hand while it was reattached. Just before the ship re-entered the shed, both the port aft guys tore their attaching toggle-flaps, which meant it had to be manoeuvred in using the remaining guys and its 'ear'.

Undeterred, the Kingsnorth team set about modifying the system with a view to trying again.

MOORING-OUT OF AIRSHIPS

As well as construction, experiments on the most efficient method of mooring-out for airships were also being undertaken and Wing Commander Usborne sent an interim report to the Inspecting Captain of Aircraft at the Central Air Offices in Sheerness on 28 September 1915. This report gave the pros and cons of pivot mooring and broadside mooring, with detailed descriptions of both systems.

DESCENDING ON TO WATER

The object of this experiment was to ascertain what difficulties would be encountered in designing a ship that could land on and moor in relatively shallow water.

In April 1915, the skids of *SS1* were fitted with inflatable fabric floats instead of wheels and had a grapnel attached. With a wind of approximately 3mph and at a height of about 150ft above the surface of the Medway, the ship's engine was shut off and it descended on to the water. The ship floated satisfactorily. The grapnel was then dropped and the ship, now significantly lighter, rose into the air and rode on the grapnel rope.

The next thing to ascertain was whether the operation could be reversed, so the grapnel was pulled in. The weight of the grapnel lowered the ship back on to the water, some ballast was dropped overboard, the ship ascended, the engine was started by turning the propeller by hand from the port skid and a good landing ashore was then made. The only difficult part of the operation had been the stowing of the wet grapnel and rope when they were pulled in.

TOWING OF AIRSHIPS BY SURFACE CRAFT

Experiments on towing airships were carried out to see if it would be possible to refuel and change crew at sea, thus increasing the airship's range of operations.

The first attempt was made in November 1914 with the Astra-Torres airship. Matching the speed of the SS *Princess Victoria*, the airship dropped a towrope from 300ft above the deck. Wind speed was measured at 15mph. The rope was successfully caught and made fast but no further trials took place until March 1916, when part of the landing ground at Kingsnorth was marked out to represent the afterdeck of a destroyer. A Coastal-class airship dropped a trail rope within the marking and the ground crew made it fast in the same way as would have been done at sea.

Having done successful trials on land, the experiment was moved to Harwich harbour, where *C1* was taken in tow by the cruiser *Carysfort*, and four days later another successful experiment was carried out at sea while the *Carysfort* was travelling at a speed of 20 knots. These tests were directed by Commodore R.Y. Tyrwhitt, and he was so impressed with the pilot's handling of the airship that he reported that in his opinion the crew had such perfect control of their ship that they appeared to be able to do what they pleased with it. His praise encouraged more tests at Kingsnorth and in the Thames Estuary, where refuelling and crew exchanges were carried out successfully.

However, it was recognised that landing an airship on a quarterdeck needed ideal weather conditions and that these were rare in the North Sea. Other methods of exchange needed to be developed for such situations.

An SS airship landing on the deck of a submarine. Precision flying and calm conditions were vital to prevent any member of the minimal 'ground crew' being swept overboard. Second in a set of three photographs. (Fleet Air Arm Museum 1981/051/0006)

The Coastal airship was then raised to a height of 100ft and the crew exchange was effected by use of a bosun's chair. The airship was then refuelled. Sixty gallons of fuel were transferred vertically into the airship's fuel tanks in just eight minutes, using compressed air to force the fuel up the hose from a tank situated on the cruiser's deck.

AIRSHIP/AEROPLANE HYBRID – AIRSHIPLANE *AP1*

Zeppelin bombing raids, which began in January 1915, prompted Wing Commander Usborne, Kingsnorth's station commander, to turn his ingenuity towards an effective countermeasure. His idea was to have a detachable aeroplane with wings slung beneath the balloon, which could cruise at altitude for long periods and be ready to attack the enemy as soon as they were spotted, with no need to take off and climb to the necessary height. The idea looked sound on paper and the first flight trial took place on 12 August 1915. This was successful and after a few adjustments the second and third test flights took place on 23 and 31 August, during which everything seemed to go well. The rigging was grouped so it came to three points on a horizontal line, one attached in front of the propeller, one just behind the pilot's seat and the third near the stern of the car.

Between September and October, the slipping mechanism was tested and modified. In tests the forward slip was the last to go, but the time between this and the other two was less than a second. A more complex system was devised but there were problems with faulty safety catches. In November a new system of suspension was tried out, the aeroplane's weight being distributed over the length of the envelope by means of a built-up wooden girder above it.

Tragedy struck on 21 February 1916 when Wing Commander Usborne and Squadron Commander Ireland took the 'airshiplane' up for another test after some minor alterations. The airship took off and circled up, ascending to a height of about 4,000ft. Suddenly something went wrong with the detachment gear, and people on the ground saw the aircraft fall in a side-slip, turning over as it fell. Commander Ireland was thrown out into the River Medway before the machine crashed to the ground in the Strood railway goods yard. Commander Usborne was still strapped in his seat. It was presumed he had struggled to gain control of the machine to the end. Both men were killed. A commission of enquiry was held on the accident and found that the craft had exceeded its equilibrium height. This had caused a loss of pressure in the envelope, which triggered the premature release of the forward suspension. The weight of the engine pulled the aeroplane down at the front and the remaining suspension wires snapped, damaging some of the aeroplane controls as it fell, thus making Commander Usborne's attempts to regain control futile.

The experiment was discontinued as far as non-rigid airships were concerned, though the idea was tried again at a later date, and with more success, using a rigid airship.

As well as airship development, the team at Kingsnorth were working on the support of the service looking at designs for mooring masts, portable hangars, mobile workshops and equipment for the recovery of airships from inaccessible places.

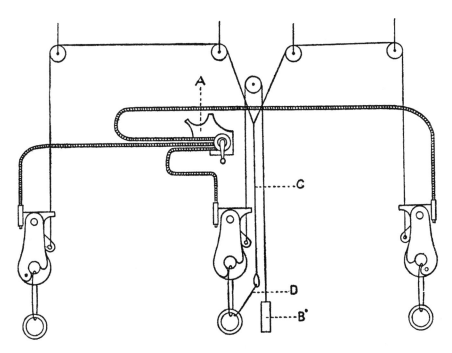

Illustration of the original slipping mechanism from the 'Airship Experimental Report 1915', showing how one toggle, 'B', released all three catches together. (RAF Museum, Hendon)

The view from below as the 'airshiplane' rose for a test flight. (Fleet Air Arm Museum A/Ships 301)

VARIATIONS ON THE BASIC DESIGN OF THE SS AIRSHIPS

In his book, *Airship Pilot No. 28*, Captain T.B. Williams describes a few incidents relating to experiments for improving the performance of the SS-class airships between July and November 1916. During this time he was captain of the airship *SS31*, affectionately known as the 'Flying Bedstead'. This airship was fitted with a pusher engine in the rear, which gave it a tendency to travel almost sideways. Even official reports described *SS31* as being fitted with a Maurice Farman or 'Bedstead' car. The pusher engine improved the view but the steering was sluggish and stiff. These shortcomings made it a favourite for testing improvements, as well as being used for pilot training.

SS14, captained by S.E. Taylor was also used for experimentation as well as training. On one occasion, Taylor, assisted by Williams, took *SS14* on a test flight with a newly fitted water-cooled Curtiss engine. As they descended, they discovered the engine had developed a leak. They throttled back but this didn't prevent the engine from seizing up. They could do little but drift as the engine cooled, before taking turns going out on the skids to hand-start the engine. Failing to get the engine to start, they settled down beside the churchyard at Hoo. Tethering the airship by the graves, they went into a local shop and obtained some chewing gum to stop the leak, filled the radiator from the village pump and succeeded in starting the engine without

The original 'Flying Bedstead', *SS31* at Kingsnorth. (Fleet Air Arm Museum 1994/096/0021)

any problem. Having lost gas, and lift, Taylor flew the ship back to Kingsnorth alone. Williams phoned the base to let them know the situation before walking back.

On another occasion, SS14 was fitted with an experimental rudder situated on top of the envelope. This arrangement proved most unsatisfactory and considerable difficulty was experienced in returning to the landing ground.

SS31 made a number of balloon/unpowered landings when engine experiments failed, highlighting the need for aeronautical training in ballooning as well as powered flight.

On one occasion a new type of suspension lacing was fitted. After a cautious circuit of the air station, one of the lacings carried away, releasing the main starboard suspension, which whipped back and broke the starboard elevator control wire. This in turn cut through the propeller blades 'like carrots'. Luckily the envelope was not pierced and Williams had shut the throttle at the first sign of trouble, so once the series of breakages had finished, his out-of-balance engine was just ticking over and he was able to set the ship down with minimal damage, despite the fact he was half lying on his side. Captain Taylor was assisting Williams on this occasion and both were fortunate to escape injury.

Lieutenant Cave-Brown-Cave was continually frustrated with problems caused by the need to adapt aeroplane engines that had never been designed for the slow speeds and long running times required for airship operation. He was, reputedly, complaining bitterly about the unsuitability of these engines and as a consequence of these complaints his commanding officer told him to 'Get out and get a proper engine made'. The lieutenant responded promptly. Taking the train to Derby, he requested a meeting with Henry Royce. The subsequent discussion of airship-engine requirements took two hours. As a result of this meeting, Rolls-Royce produced the 75hp Hawk engine, which was reliable at the slowest speeds, once the inevitable teething troubles had been sorted out.

COVERT AIRSHIP OPERATIONS

The War Office was interested in the possibility of using airships in covert operations to scout enemy positions on land and drop men behind enemy lines. They hoped that an airship flying over enemy lines at night would be able to go undetected. The experiments were started at Polegate, where W.P.C. Chambers and Victor Goddard used SS13 to identify potential problems for night flying. The Kingsnorth team were instructed to paint the car of SS40, which had just been supplied by Armstrong Whitworth, matte black, fit it with a black envelope and send it to Polegate, where Chambers and Goddard fitted a silencer to the engine, created special hooded landing lights and devised a method whereby the identification roundels could be hidden when over enemy lines. War Office representatives were given a demonstration on the night of 30 May 1916.

Orders arrived for Chambers and Goddard to embark with this airship, a portable silicol gas plant and the minimum technical support staff, a party of twenty men including Chambers and Goddard. Having crossed the Channel on 7 July 1916, they proceeded to a quiet village near the town of Freyvent, where they were told to familiarise themselves with the area. On 8 August 1916, Goddard was ordered to take *SS40* back to England to have the envelope enlarged at Kingsnorth. Lieutenant Robbins used it for parachute experiments.

Upon returning to France, the airship was declared operational and two trained observers from the RFC joined the team to make night-time observation flights over enemy lines. The RFC men were not happy working with a large quantity of highly inflammable gas above their heads. It turned out that volunteers for missions behind enemy lines felt the same so no volunteers came forward to be dropped and collected by airship. Ironically the German gunners had been expressly forbidden to fire on airships, having mistakenly shot down a couple of their own Zeppelins.

SS40 returned to Kingsnorth on 22 October 1916. While stationed there she apparently disappeared from time to time doing covert night work, leaving Kingsnorth for good on 27 March 1917. One of the SSP airships, *SS2* or *SS5*, was similarly modified in May 1917 to accompany the British Expeditionary Force but the project was cancelled as it was decided to use aeroplanes instead. Thus died the 'stealth' airship. Though it had only a brief life, it was possibly the first stealth aircraft in British military history.

By the middle of 1916, the Kingsnorth team were looking for a new Submarine Scout design that would provide improved performance and greater comfort for the crew. The result was the SSP class, which had a longer car that could carry three men: a pilot, a wireless operator and an engineer. They were powered by a pusher engine, with the air scoop for the ballonets located in the slipstream.

The movement of personnel meant that officers who had trained at Kingsnorth were used to an environment which encouraged innovation. Many of them were involved in modifying the ships they flew and Lieutenant F.M. Rope was influential in designing the SSZ airship at Capal, which superseded the SSP just five months after it went into production. The first SSZs were built at several stations, many at Wormwood Scrubs, before production of the last batch was transferred to Kingsnorth.

COASTAL- AND NORTH SEA-CLASS AIRSHIPS

Following the successful design of the Submarine Scout airships, the team at Kingsnorth were asked to design larger, non-rigid ships which would have a longer range, a larger carrying capacity and increased reliability. This work was being carried out at the same time as the improvements on the Submarine Scouts. For the car, the Kingsnorth team again decided to adapt an aeroplane fuselage, as these could be easily procured and would speed up production. Two twin-cockpit Avro 510 seaplane bodies were joined to produce a four-seater car powered by two 150-horsepower Sunbeam engines at either end of the car. The forward engine was set up in the normal configuration as a tractor engine and the aft engine was fitted with a pusher screw. The first trial flight of the first Coastal airship took place on 26 May 1915, which, along with further trials, led to various modifications, including strengthening of the nose cone, changing the landing skids and altering the radiator on the aft engine.

Increasing the size of the airship also increased its carrying capacity, enabling them to be armed with two large bombs or depth charges weighing 230lb. Alternatively they could carry four smaller bombs. In addition to their offensive weapons, they were fitted with two Lewis guns for defence. One could be mounted at various places on the car and the other was mounted on

C1 at Kingsnorth, May 1915. (Fleet Air Arm Museum A/SHIP 121)

Coastal 23 being prepared for a test flight. All of the airships built at Kingsnorth were rigorously tested before being sent out. (Imperial War Museum HU_128830)

a platform on top of the envelope and reached via a tube that ran vertically through the centre of the envelope.

These airships proved as popular as the smaller ones but the navy wanted even larger ships for long-range work. The Kingsnorth designers began drawing up specifications for an even bigger class of ship that would cover this, while Vickers designed and built even bigger rigid airships at Barrow.

The North Sea-class airship was based on a modified form of the Astra-Torres design. Initial flight trials of the first NS airship took place on 2 February 1917. This trial showed a major problem caused by increasing the size of the ship. It had become accepted practice to sling the fuel tanks on either side of the envelope, an excellent arrangement for the smaller airships. However the size of the North Sea-class ship necessitated much longer pipes between the tanks and the engine. During the trial flight, these copper fuel pipes fractured, due to the exaggeration of the engine vibrations along the length of the pipe, causing petrol to leak down the outside of the pipes and over the hot engines. Lieutenant Commander Robinson was forced to make an emergency landing and used three of his ballast sandbags to extinguish the resulting fire.

The second North Sea airship to be built was undergoing trials on 16 June 1917 when it crash-landed at Stoneham, near Stowmarket, badly damaging the envelope in the process. The cause of this accident was also linked to the

NS4 at Kingsnorth, 17 October 1918. Barton's Farm buildings can be seen in the background. (Fleet Air Arm Museum A/SHIP 115)

increased size of the ship. The complex arrangement of gears and linkages on the drive shafts that ran between the engines and the propellers was found to be prone to disintegration at speed.

The engineering officer Lieutenant Commander Andrew S. Abell and his team had to find ways around these problems. By this time, the Kingsnorth team were working with other establishments and, in January 1918, J.R. Pannell AMIME and R. Jones MA, at Cranmore, produced a lengthy report on one of these experiments on a model of the airship.

Coastal Star airships were developed and built at Kingsnorth as an interim measure while problems with the North Sea design were being ironed out. A new design of envelope and improvements to the car, including plywood cladding with glass portholes and a glass panel in the floor, were made, though the car was still open at the top.

The engineers' drawing office would have been heavily involved in the design process, creating lift diagrams for the ships, calculating the weight of the fabric and every attachment to the ship, planes, valves, gun platform, nose-stiffening, Eta patches, ballonets and so on, then taking these off from the lift outline. This was a complex and lengthy process; a 'plane' that existed only in drawings had to have its weight calculated from the drawings often down to the smallest part.

All the twenty-seven Coastal-class airships, ten Coastal Stars and seventeen North Sea airships were constructed at Kingsnorth.

ARMAMENTS

Bombs

The idea of using airships to drop bombs came right at the beginning of their development, and tests on a large number of bombs of different types took place in May 1915. There were small incendiary bombs – such as Groves Incendiary Candles, about the size of a roman candle – and Rankin Arrows, which were designed as anti-airship missiles, up to 500lb bombs filled with troytal, an early Eastern European form of TNT. Ways of improving the effectiveness of these bombs were explored and anti-submarine bombs with delay fuses that would burn underwater were also tried, as well as various methods of delivery for different sizes of bomb.

Guns

The preferred gun for use on SS-class airships was a light Maxim, with a mounting on each side of the ship so the gun could be moved to whichever side it was needed. Experiments regarding a suspended mounting to use a Lewis Gun on an SS ship were tried on *SS14*.

The Coastal airships were usually fitted with Lewis Guns, produced under licence by the Birmingham Small Arms Co. Ltd. These automatic machine guns fired British .303 rounds at a rate of 5–600 rounds per minute from round drum magazines, the small drums holding forty-seven rounds and the large drums ninety-seven rounds. Before the guns were fitted, experiments took place to ensure they were safe if there was a hydrogen leak.

In August 1917, experiments were carried out to explore the possibility of these airships carrying larger guns. A long and a short version of the Hotchkiss 37mm revolving cannon was tried, as was a Vickers Mark IV and 1.59-inch QF Airo guns. These were mounted in a cage sunk into a recess in the airship envelope and supported with internal ties, but no external skid.

The Hotchkiss revolving cannon consisted of five revolving barrels worked by a simple and robust screw mechanism. They were capable of firing forty-three rounds per minute from compact, ten-round feed magazines. The navy had been using them against torpedo boats for many years. The blast of both types of Hotchkiss guns damaged the fabric of the airship envelope.

Vickers Mark IV QF 4in naval gun was introduced in 1911 as a fast-loading light gun and was the main gun on most Royal Navy destroyers, where it was used as a submarine gun firing 4in (101.6mm) shells weighing 31lb (14.06kg). The Vickers 1.59in QF Airo gun was commonly known as the Vickers-Crayford rocket gun because the incendiary it fired had two apertures at the

Gun emplacement at top of airship envelope. (Imperial War Museum HU_128828)

base which emitted flames. It is more likely that the ammunition tested for airship use would have been the armour-piercing, high-explosive cartridges. The Vickers 1.59 did not puncture the fabric of the airship envelope, even when fired in contact with it.

PARACHUTES

Spencer and Calthrop parachutes were tested at Kingsnorth in 1915. Mr Spencer demonstrated his parachute, making a successful jump from *No. 3* airship at a height of about 1,000ft. The experimental team then dropped three parachutes from a kite balloon 400ft up and filmed the descent of each with a cine-camera to enable them to watch the descent several times and thus aid accurate comparisons.

ENVELOPE-PATCHING DEVICE

Ingenious solutions to problems were always being sought and in the experimental department's bulletin of April 1917 are a description and diagrams for an envelope-patching device based on the same technology as that utilised by an umbrella. By September, this device for rapidly closing a hole in the airship envelope had been built and photographs of the operation and test results were published.

BEHAVIOUR OF ENVELOPES UNDER PRESSURE

On 27 May 1917, an experiment was carried out:

> by increasing pressure in Coastal envelope until internal curtains gave way and envelope turned from a trilobe form into cigar shape. Finally the rigging

Mr Spencer, on the left, with Mr McWade, inside a Coastal airship envelope, ballonet inflated. (RAF Museum Archive, Hendon AC78/27/17)

was drawn through the envelope causing a split of about 6ft long. From this it appears that if a Coastal Airship was by accident taken to an extreme height the envelope would not burst, but might split at the bottom and descend as a free balloon. This officer [Wing Commander Cave-Brown-Cave] went inside the envelope to witness the effects of the pressure.

SELF-SEALING FUEL TANKS

In January 1917, Kingsnorth was one of several places researching self-sealing fuel tanks that would resist incendiary ammunition. Their design consisted of a 20-gallon bag of airship envelope fabric sealed with a special petrol-proof nitro-cellulose dope. This was enclosed within a second bag of ¼in-thick grey rubber. The bags were then encased for support in a box made of four-ply wood with duralumin angles at the corners. The whole tank weighed 54lb.

The tank was sent to the Armament Experimental Station for testing, where it was shot at with three bursts of fire using a mixture of ammunition, and was described as 'efficient in its self-sealing properties'. They commented that it was rather heavy, but a greater concern became apparent when they opened the tank twenty-four hours later and found the rubber could be torn easily and split if bent. Further tests included increasing the internal pressure in the tank until the wooden box split at a pressure of 15lb/sq. in. However, the internal fabric bag did not rupture. The problem with the degradation of the rubber when exposed to petrol was found to be reversible if the bag was removed from the wooden case, in a well-ventilated area, and the petrol was allowed to dry out of the rubber completely.

In May 1918, it was decided that the hydrogen-filled airship envelope was more likely to be hit than the petrol tanks and that the weight of the self-sealing tanks was too great to make them worth fitting to an airship. Thus no further experiments were required at Kingsnorth.

MINESWEEPING

During the first months of 1919, experiments took place with *NS16* on the use of airships to sweep for mines. The great advantage of using airships as minesweepers was that they could not accidentally touch the mines and blow themselves up. However, there was, inevitably, a technical difficulty that needed to be solved before the airships could be employed in this work. The minesweeping hawser was so heavy that when it was towed through the water, the strain on the frame of the airship was too great. When lighter hawsers were tried it was found that they were not strong enough to tear the mines from their anchorage. Eventually a hawser that was not too heavy but had sufficient strength for the job was found. The *Daily Express* reported, on Saturday 21 June, that airships would be used to clear the estimated 50,000 mines from the 5,000 square miles of sea between the Shetland Isles and the Norwegian coast.

GAS PRODUCTION

The chemical laboratories were also involved in a lot of experimental work. Trials of the new silicol plant, erected by Vickers, commenced at midnight on 4 November 1914. An inadequate water supply, caused by a variety of factors, prevented the equipment from working properly. Discussions were held with the superintending civil engineer and Mr Weekes of Vickers, who proposed building a large tank into the water system to steady the supply and prevent silting up. Drainage of waste water was another element of the process that needed to be dealt with. Commander Usborne also noted that the clothing of the men taking part in the trial had been damaged by the chemicals used in gas production and requested a supply of adequate clothing for these men.

Given the problems with silt, ways of reusing the waste water were considered. One of the problems involved in the reuse of this water was that it contained a considerable amount of phosphine in solution. This is highly poisonous and is also undesirable in the hydrogen, but it can be removed by blowing air through the water, or by exposing the water to air in quite deep pools. Reusing the water was thought to be a good idea and the possibilities of using a cooling tower for this were considered in 1915.

Production of hydrogen by the silicol process involves a reaction of silicon with hot concentrated caustic-soda solution, the by-product of this process being sodium silicate ('waterglass'). The generating equipment was simple: a stirred reaction vessel and a scrubber to remove steam and some water-soluble impurities, which gave 99 per cent pure hydrogen. A relatively small plant could produce 2,000–2,500ft^3 of gas per hour. Very large quantities of water were required for reaction, scrubbing and cooling, though much of this requirement could be seawater.

As the sodium silicate and other by-products formed a sludge, which rapidly solidified in the reactor, batch operation was necessary to enable regular cleaning of the equipment. Gas generation, purification and feed to the hangars would have been at a fairly low pressure, but local storage tanks were up to 600 psi and cylinders for distant use were compressed up to 1,800 psi. Ferrosilicon containing 90 per cent silicon was commercially available, as was caustic soda. Heating would have been coal-fired.

The use of chemical gas as a weapon was also being considered, the brief being to find a poisonous gas that would kill quickly and humanely, thus replacing chlorine gas, which caused acute suffering. In 1915 Lieutenant Brock and Mr Macleod performed a series of experiments to ascertain the effects of asphyxiating and life-destroying chemical gases for offensive use. Experiments were also undertaken in defence against gas attacks. Various substances were exploded in the vicinity of pigs, sheep and rabbits under the authority of Commander Wilton.

In December 1916, Mr Arthur R. Griggs was appointed chief chemist in the hydrogen laboratory at Kingsnorth. For the next two years he was employed in the production of hydrogen using both the silicol and the water-gas processes. The latter became the standard industrial method of producing hydrogen in large quantities. Steam was reduced to hydrogen by passing it over metallic iron at a high temperature. The iron oxide produced in this reaction was converted back to active iron by water gas, a mixture of carbon monoxide and hydrogen obtained by passing steam over incandescent coke. Gas purification was essential. Production costs were low but skilled operators were needed to run the plant almost continuously. The combination of large, complex and expensive fixed plant and skilled operators meant that only a few large airship stations had this kind of plant. The Kingsnorth water gas plant was being built at the beginning of 1917. Although the chemicals involved were not as toxic as those used in the silicol process, the operators still had problems with exposure to the hydrogen gas.

In November 1918, preparations for a new electrolytic plant were underway to replace the water gas plant. A recommendation was made that this project be completed as both hydrogen and oxygen would be required and the new plant would be more economical to run. (It is not clear from my research whether the new plant was built, but as experimental work at the station was still ongoing in June 1920 it may well have been.)

AIRSHIP FABRICS

The laboratory not only tested the quality of the hydrogen but did a considerable amount of work on research to 'produce a fabric of low weight, high tensile strength and low permeability to hydrogen'. The laboratory employed a staff of seven, who spent much of their time conducting routine tests on materials to ensure they met Admiralty specifications, and experiments with rubber and dopes to improve balloon fabric. Apparatus for applying dope using a spray were considered a great improvement, enabling the dope to be applied quickly and evenly, with the added advantage that it greatly reduced the heavy waste to which earlier application methods were prone. From the earliest days of the station, the Kingsnorth chemists tested different recipes for dope, and the best proportions of rubber and dope to use in envelope construction. Doping improved gas-tightness but added to weight, and early dopes also made the fabric more flammable, problems which needed to be addressed urgently. New dopes based on cellulose nitrate and cellulose acetate were tested. The latter was flame-resistant but cracked when dry. Dope paints for painting identification markings and camouflage had to be developed as normal paint was found to destroy the gas-tight properties of the underlying material. This work was considered so important that a laboratory specialising in dope research was authorised to be built at Kingsnorth in 1915.

A report on the superiority of 'stuck' over sewn seams was submitted on 27 May 1918.

Reducing the weight attached to balloons was always a challenge and by April 1916 the Kingsnorth chemists had developed a fabric petrol tank. It was tested over the next five months ready for use in the North Sea-class airships.

A document from the Director of Research on work planned or in progress at the chemical laboratory was submitted on 21 June 1920. It included weathering of airship fabrics at Kingsnorth and, in Egypt, tests on the tearing strength of different configurations of two-ply envelope fabric. The gas permeability of various fabrics and hydrogen purity were all being worked on at this time also.

The development of elastic shock absorbers was another of the projects on which the laboratory worked. This involved collecting information on a large number of types of elastic cord.

CAMOUFLAGE

There were a number of ideas relating to the painting of the airship envelope to camouflage it, including the ones painted black for night flying. However the most extraordinary idea was to enable the airship crew to create an artificial cloud within which the airship could hide. There were several problems that had to be overcome. The cloud had to stay around the ship while it was moving, not trail behind it like the wake of a boat; it had to be breathable or the crew would expire within it; and the components needed to be transported in light containers. Experiment C9, described in the 1915 annual report, shows that one of the combinations tried was ammonia and chlorine, which produced dense white clouds of ammonium chloride. However as this is an irritant I can't imagine that it would have proved suitable!

Kingsnorth 25 April 1917 showing Sparrow Castle, which housed the telephone exchange, dwarfed by the electricity-generating station behind it on the left, one of the two hydrogen stations behind it and the boiler house on the right behind the lower garage building that faced the road. The two large tanks are for hydrogen. Beyond the boiler house is the electricity-generating station, a huge dark cooling tower, the older of the hydrogen-generating stations and stores buildings. To the right of the stores you can just see rows of hydrogen cylinders. The pair of low buildings to the right of the cylinders housed the drawing office and on the right of that is the rubber dope laboratory. In the foreground, opposite Sparrow Castle, are two blocks of garages, which give an indication of the number of vehicles used on site. (Fleet Air Arm A/STN 304)

3

OPERATIONS AND PROCEDURES

Land, sheds, accommodation, infrastructure and transport were all provided to support one thing – airship development. However, experimental work and large-scale production of airships were not the only tasks undertaken at Kingsnorth. A considerable number of airship pilots were provided with their basic training at this facility and the day-to-day operation of the station involved a wide range of tasks.

SECURITY

On 7 February 1914, Winston Churchill, First Lord of the Admiralty, visited RN air stations at Grain, Eastchurch and Kingsnorth. Airships and station staff had yet to arrive and there was only one watchman guarding the place at night and over the weekends. Churchill was concerned that the wooden shed would be a target for an incendiary attack, not by enemy spies but by suffragettes, who were becoming extremely militant. He asked that security be increased.

Once the station staff was up to strength, one of the least exciting tasks for ordinary airmen, particularly those with any military training, was guard duty. These duties were organised to the same timetable as naval watches:

First watch	8 p.m.–midnight
Middle watch	Midnight–4 a.m.
Morning watch	4 a.m.–8 a.m.
Forenoon watch	8 a.m.–noon
Afternoon watch	Noon–4 p.m.
First dog watch	4 p.m.–6 p.m.
Second dog watch	6 p.m.–8 p.m.

There were four men in each guard and the watches were four hours on and eight hours off. The dog watches ensured the same man wasn't on the same watch every time. Every four days there was a break of thirty-two hours, which coincided with a weekend once a month.

Guard duties consisted of examining civilian passes, safeguarding government property, challenging anyone approaching at night (if there was no reply to the third challenge, guards were expected to fire on the intruder) and, of course, giving the proper salute to all officers, as befitted their rank. All the stations had a fair number of civilians coming and going, engaged in delivering goods and building maintenance, added to which Kingsnorth also had a large civilian workforce that came in every day and would have been well known to the guards. Military personnel also had passes, which had to be checked as they came and went.

Middle watches were cold and hungry, especially in the winter months. There was little shelter from the cold winds, it was near impossible to march up and down the whole of the watch, and if one stood still the cold seeped through even the thickest layers of clothing. The main interruption to the monotony of night watches was not a welcome one – air raids. Although the raiders did not bomb the stations on the Hoo Peninsula, the anti-aircraft fire and resulting shrapnel could be dangerous to anyone out in the open. What goes up must come down, and many a sentry in his box heard the clatter as a random piece of spent armaments bounced off the roof above his head.

During November 1914, plans were put in place regarding what would happen at Kingsnorth in the event of an enemy invasion. Safe places for the airships to be moved to were identified, and systems were put in place for immediately required stores and personnel to be moved by road and less urgent equipment to be moved by rail via Gravesend. Defence of the airship sheds and deployment of the airships for artillery-spotting were also covered.

These plans were amended in 1917, about the time Commander P. Harrington Edwards arrived at the station. There was serious talk of a German invasion and the orders for Kingsnorth regarding what should be done if this occurred changed. New orders were to withdraw valuable plant, and for RNAS personnel to stand and fight. Detailed plans and practices regarding how this would work, so everyone knew what their role would be if the order was given, were evolved. This added excitement, but also uncertainty, to the routine work that had been the norm up until now.

DRILLS, PARADES AND ASSEMBLIES

As with all military establishments, drill and parades were regular features of the day for every serviceman and officer. Assemblies were called when needed so that announcements could be made to all the men at once.

The most popular of these assemblies was the one called to announce the long-awaited Armistice. News of peace was followed by a day of celebration with spontaneous singing. Many people celebrated in fancy dress, and after lunch practically the entire station staff descended on Hoo. The party returned to the station, bringing many villagers with it, and continued until everyone was hoarse.

DISCIPLINE

Station discipline used the same principles as discipline aboard a navy vessel. Off-duty men going off-base had to apply for permission to 'go ashore' and punishment for the infringement of regulations was also conducted along Admiralty guidelines. One of the commonest forms of punishment was the lock-up, known by the men as the 'rattle', the threat of which seems to have impressed some men more than others.

The fact that there were civilian staff and army personnel on the base made discipline issues a lot more complex than had the staff consisted entirely of navy men. The formation of the Royal Air Force did little to simplify the situation in the early days of its existence, as the interpretation of new regulations often needed clarification.

There was also a certain amount of leeway given to airship pilots, it having been recognised that the stress these men were under needed release from time to time. This was, however, only tolerated on the base and one officer was ignominiously discharged for being drunk 'on shore'.

Any officer absent without leave could also expect a serious reprimand and the likelihood of returning to the ranks.

THEFTS

Despite the consequences of being caught, thefts on the base did occur. When this involved thefts from the men's quarters, suspicions were rife and traps were set to catch the culprit. There was a humorous description of a bungled attempt to catch a thief in the June 1917 edition of *Flighty*, the station magazine, which has been included in the chapter on personnel. Petty pilfering generally would have been a problem.

COMMUNICATIONS

Procedures regarding communication between the airship station at Kingsnorth and Commander E.A. Masterman RN was the subject of a dispatch on 1 April 1914, but newly appointed Station Commander N.F. Usborne was not provided with clear instructions regarding this, leading to some pithy letters between himself and the Inspecting Captain of Aircraft at Sheerness in July 1914.

Communications were becoming increasingly important. On 5 August 1914, Lieutenant Lefroy arrived at Kingsnorth with wireless equipment to enable airships to communicate with ships and ground crews. Given the problem of engine noise, crews may have had to turn off the engines in order to hear incoming radio messages, although outward messages did not present such a problem.

The ability to communicate by wireless telegraph did not solve communication problems immediately, as the procedures for communication were not clear. On the Parseval airship's first patrol, Captain J.N. Fletcher and his crew were under orders to maintain wireless silence, except for the purpose of reporting hostile activity. They ignored a message, 'P4 report', and were presumed to have been lost, so their report of a flotilla of small ships laying mines was not received because their frequency was no longer being monitored. As dawn broke, they returned. Crossing the Kent coast, they were fired on by a division of the Territorial Army, despite the fact that they were flying a huge White Ensign to identify them as a British airship. It turned out that the mine-layers were, in fact, minesweepers that had not been included on the 'dispositions' list. The flight showed up so many shortcomings in procedure that all airship flights were cancelled while things were sorted out.

Although airships carried bombs to drop on enemy submarines, their chief function was the detection and report of enemy craft to the local senior naval officer, who would send out a suitable vessel to intercept and engage the enemy. It was essential that, on receipt of a report, the position of the airship should be known so that attacking vessels knew where to concentrate their hunt. To aid airship captains in pinpointing their location, the Admiralty ordered a network of wireless direction-finding stations around the coast to be erected by the Marconi company in August 1915. There were two kinds of station: some could transmit to a range of 150 miles, others were simple receiving stations that were used to get a cross-bearing and plot the position of airships using the call sign they sent out once an hour.

TRANSPORT

As well as the standard- and narrow-gauge railway lines, the station had a number of road vehicles. There were at least two lorries, some kind of bus or charabanc which transported men on shore leave into town, and at least one car used by the officers.

There were several garages on site where these vehicles were stored and maintained by driver-mechanics and repair hands. In June 1917, *Flighty* contained a quick snippet regarding a family of sparrows being raised in a corner of the London General Omnibus Company lorry while it was in for repairs. Someone must have been a keen ornithologist with a persuasive argument or the lorry was not needed for the duration of the raising of the chicks.

GAS-RELATED DANGERS

Production of gas by the silicol method involved the use of caustic soda. The hydrogen workers needed to wear protective clothing and any man who had to work underneath the plant also needed to wear a protective face mask.

Impurities in the gas were also a danger. Not only could they have a detrimental effect on the lift available to the ship, but some reacted with dye on weather-resistant cordage, forming acids that rotted the rope fibres.

Fire was a serious danger from the first, as hydrogen, the doped material envelopes that held it and the wooden construction of the car holding the airship crew were all very flammable. One of the greatest risks was that of a fire within the airship shed during inflation of the ballonets, and procedures to combat fire were very important. On 29 June 1914, Commander Usborne reported to the commanding officer of the Naval Airship Section directly, regarding a serious fire that had taken place the day before:

At 8.45 p.m. on 28th instant, the inflation of No.3 airship was in progress, and nearly finished, in the iron shed.

I was inside the shed. Certain hands were under the ship and the usual party were working the bottles. These latter were stacked on the north side of the iron shed, a few feet distant from it, valve ends being towards it.

A sentry was stationed at the door where the filling hose entered the shed. Immediately above the hose was a piece of canvas, filled with about half a ton of earth, so supported that when the sentry cut a strand, this load would fall on the hose and prevent any possible fire which might originate from spreading into the shed.

At 8.45 p.m. I heard shouts outside and saw the sentry drop the load of earth. The hose was not squashed by it, so I seized the hose and was surprised to find the pressure in it was very great. I had difficulty in squeezing it so as to stop the flow of gas. (Note: previously the pressure had been very small).

The construction of the hose caused the pipe to burst outside the shed, thus disconnecting it. At the same time I shouted to the men under the airship to come out, and cut the hose inside the shed, thus making a complete break in it.

This being done, i.e. about a minute after the outbreak I was able to let go of the hose I was holding. I directed the men in the shed to clear out and get beyond the shed door. I then looked out of the little side door and saw that the fire was of large dimensions. A large number of bottles, perhaps 80, were discharging jets of burning gas, various hosepipes were burning fiercely, and two baulks of timber on which the working party had been standing had caught. Three men were trying ineffectually to put the fire out from a distance with 'Pyrene'.

Judging that it was impossible to put the gas out and that there was immediate danger of the stack of bottles exploding (owing to the flames raising the pressure in the bottles and at the same time weakening the bottles locally, where the jets of flame impinged on them) I directed the men working there to join the remainder under cover.

Cover was obtained by sitting down behind the massive part which constituted the bottom of the sliding doors.

Occasional glances told me of the progress of the fire. After some ten or fifteen minutes it appeared to have abated, and I approached it. Six bottles were still burning feebly; these were smothered in earth. The burning timber &c., was put out with 'Pyrene'.

It was noticed that the bottles were hot right through to their bases. Not only those bottles which were turned on had caught; others which were not turned on were burning round the valve spindles &c..

The origin of the fire was the spontaneous ignition of one jet on being turned on. The air appears to have contained sufficient gas to cause the immediate ignition within reach.

If the ignition had taken place within the wooden shed its total destruction is probable.

I was able to complete the inflation this morning in slow time using 6 separate tubes at a time.

I am taking steps today to obtain a nine way set of High Pressure inflation gear for carrying out topping-up.

Last Summer during the absence of the s.o. on duty a few trifling jets of flame occurred at Farnborough. I sent a report there to the Admiralty; and those experiences led to the great precautions taken on this occasion. I understand that a few weeks ago a fire occurred at Farnborough of similar origin, but such that the men were just able to get it under control.

This is the third and worst of these fires. There appears to be no doubt that fire can be prevented by the use of a H.P. filling system.

I therefore submit (a) that the permanent piping arrangements for this station may be hastened. (b) That H.P. connections for the bottles may be provided.

I respectfully submit that, unless provided with written orders or in case of war emergency, I am not prepared to allow any ship to be inflated at this station under my command, except with H.P. connections, or other safe system.

Papers confirming the installation of high-pressure connections for inflating airships have yet to come to light but work on airships continued, presumably with improved safety precautions, as on 24 July 1914 Wing

Commander Usborne sent in a lengthy report on an experimental flight of the Astra-Torres *AT3*.

An explosion that had tragic consequences occurred at Kingsnorth on 27 May 1917, when fire broke out in a gas holder. Wing Commander Cave-Brown-Cave and Lieutenant P.T. Armstrong discharged a considerable quantity of gas, and the leak was allowed to burn itself out. They then made an examination of the gas holder and satisfied themselves that there was no flame on the surface. Lieutenant Armstrong continued to take precautionary measures, but about twenty minutes later the holder blew up. Lieutenant Armstrong and Leading Mechanic Charles W. Harris were both killed while two other men, Petty Officer 'Jock' Beveridge and Air Mechanic Doole, were severely injured. The station commander at this time was Captain A.P. Davidson. He investigated the accident and came to the conclusion that the explosion must have been caused by a spark coming into contact with a mixture of hydrogen gas and air. An inquest on 2 June was given particulars of the explosion and a verdict of accidental death was returned in each case.

Workers in the gas plant were also at risk of suffocation and four canaries were kept there to give advanced warning of life-threatening leaks.

MANUAL HANDLING OF AIRSHIPS

Large numbers of men were needed to handle the ropes, pulling the airships out of the sheds ready for take-off, hauling them down when they came in to land and getting them safely moored or hauled back into the sheds. Airships were anchored partially inflated and were usually topped up in the shed before being towed out using groups of handling lines attached to heavy cables fore and aft. Men were also needed to support the cars to prevent them from being accidentally grounded. To avoid having to vent too much hydrogen, airships usually returned in the evening when the air was cooler. The ground crew handling the airships undertaking these operations were co-ordinated by an officer shouting orders to the widely scattered groups of men through a megaphone.

Ground crews were trained to deal with the serious risks involved but accidents did happen. On Friday 23 April 1915, William Standford was part of the ground crew trying to tether a newly arrived airship. The wind was proving too strong and they could not hold it, so were forced to let go. William was either too slow or didn't hear the order to release the rope and was dragged up into the air. By the time he realised what had happened he was too high to safely let go. He hung on to the tethering rope as the ship rolled in the high winds. The crew in the airship vented gas to try to get the airship down quickly but eventually, having hung on for nearly ten minutes, his grip gave and he fell about 500ft to his death.

The handling crew of a North Star-type airship wearing their special heavy boots. (Fleet Air Arm Museum 1982/088/0013)

OTHER ACCIDENTS

Kingsnorth, being between two major river estuaries and controlled by the Navy, had access to boats. Large boats were sometimes used for towing airships but there seem to have been smaller craft as well. The report of a drowning on 8 May 1917 suggests that the waters around the station could be treacherous. Fred Beckett, a popular gas-plant hand from Urmston near Manchester, was an expert swimmer and had played water polo for Lancashire's county team. The report does not say how he came to be in a powerless boat drifting down the River Medway, or how far out he was, but his response to this predicament was to dive into the river and attempt to swim to the shore. Despite being a strong swimmer, he failed to reach land and drowned.

AIRSHIP MAINTENANCE

The envelopes had to be regularly checked for damage. This work was carried out by the rigging crew. They wore special overalls made of smooth material (with no protruding fastenings such as hooks or buttons) and special felt shoes and, thus kitted out, they would swarm all over the inflated envelope, checking every inch for any source of leakage, such as loose parts or broken seams. The men of the rigging crew had to be keen of eye, slight of build and agile. They would not only check the outside of the envelope but crawl into the narrow spaces between the envelope and the gas cells to check the inside

Rigging crew in Proto breathing apparatus ready to enter airship envelope. (Fleet Air Arm Museum A/SHIP 36)

using electric magazine hand lamps. They had to be extremely careful using these as there was a danger that battery acid could be transferred to the envelope, causing the fabric to weaken and break. For work inside the envelope, special breathing apparatus was necessary.

Once the envelope had been checked, and before it went out on patrol, the hydrogen would be topped up by the hydrogen workers. It was very important not to overfill the envelope as overstressing weakened the fabric.

The correct storage of envelopes not in use was also important. The larvae of certain moths attacked older balloons made of goldbeater's skin. More of a problem were mice, who would nibble holes in the envelopes to make themselves a cosy weatherproof nest.

PATROLS

For the most part, Kingsnorth produced airships for use elsewhere but on 3 September 1915 Admiral J. Mallaghan at the Commander-in-Chief's Office, Chatham, put in a request to the Admiralty for three SS airships to be permanently stationed at Kingsnorth for patrol work, searching for mines and submarines in the Thames Estuary.

PROTECTION FROM THE ELEMENTS

Wing Commander Usborne's report of 24 July 1914 on an experimental flight of the Astra-Torres airship included suggestions for improvements relating to his concerns for the comfort of the ten crew members. Early military aircraft were little more than wood-and-canvas boxes, but as the airships were able to stay up between twelve and twenty-two hours – much longer than the early aeroplanes – the conditions for the crew were a serious concern. I have found two descriptions from airship crew members that demonstrate the problems on the early airships: '...conditions were cramped and confined on board, exposed to the cold and at the mercy of the elements,' says one. 'As the pilot could not leave his little bucket seat during a flight of often many hours duration, he just didn't get a meal,' says the other. 'It was also difficult to answer the call of nature.' Ingenious methods of dealing with the latter problem were contrived by the pilots, and on one occasion an airship crew that had descended to sea level were literally caught with their pants down by an enemy submarine.

EXAMINATION OF ENEMY AIRSHIPS

There was a Zeppelin raid on the night of 31 March 1916 and on its way home one of the Zeppelins was intercepted and brought down off the coast. The new Commanding Officer at Kingsnorth was telephoned to inform him of this opportunity to give the airship designers there a chance to examine the Zeppelin before it sank. Wing Commander C.R. Dane, Squadron Commander T.R. Cave-Brown-Cave, Flight Lieutenant D. Harries and the official photographer at Kingsnorth were roused at 3 a.m. and headed off to Westgate-on-Sea to meet up with the Divisional Commander of Air Stations in the Nore area.

Having driven hell-for-leather around the coast road towards Margate, by 4.45 these five men had embarked in the motorboat from Westgate Seaplane Station, headed for the spot where the Zeppelin was last reported. The weather was thick so the tongue light vessel was used as a reference point. It took about forty-five minutes to find the Zeppelin. Having reached her, it was obvious she would only float for a few minutes longer so they quickly drew alongside, gathered as much information on her construction as they could and took several photographs. As the Zeppelin was rapidly sinking, orders were given to buoy her. The motorboat was failing so they returned to the tongue light ship and were taken back to Margate.

Recommendations were made that a special enquiry should be held to gather information from the two ships that had been in the area at the time, and that their crews be asked to lend any papers or articles they might have to aid the enquiry.

If a Zeppelin was brought down on land, the procedure was very similar. The raids usually took place at night. When a ship was downed, the area was secured by the local forces and any surviving crew were detained. If the ship came down within reach of an airship base, the base would be informed and an officer would be driven down to examine the remains. His driver-mechanic would pack into the car a bedroll and a folding bicycle so that if, as was often the case, they had to wait until dawn to examine the remains, the driver-mechanic could bed down on the back seat of the car and the officer

LZ15 being examined as she slowly sank beneath the waves. (Imperial War Museum HU_128827)

could use the bike if he needed to travel any distance to find a bed for the night. The following day they would be up with the sun, remove any pieces that might be worth examining more closely and return with them for the station design team to look over and investigate further.

ADMIRALTY VISITS

On 4 August 1916, Commodore Sueter invited members of the Advisory Committee for Aeronautics to visit the RN Airship Station at Kingsnorth on the tenth of the month. In preparation for their visit, Commander Cave-Brown-Cave produced an account of work in progress:

The work in progress at the station includes:-

1.   Design and construction of all non-rigid ships.
2.   Research work on various points connected mainly with the materials used in construction.
3.   Training pilots for the Airship Branch of the R.N.A.S.
4.   Patrol and duties as required by the Commander-in-Chief.

There are normally at the station four ships engaged in routine flying and on instruction; of these, two are of the Coastal type, and two of the smaller 'SS' type. The remainder of the ships on the Station are of the Coastal type and are in process of construction.

The types of ship that have been designed at the Station and are still in general use are the 'SS' type of 63,000 cubic feet capacity. Of these 45 have been constructed, and with the exception of certain losses are at present flying at various Air Stations round the coast. The other type is the Coastal of 170,000 cubic feet capacity. Of these, 21 have already been completed at the station.

The designs of the 'N.S.' type have been completed, and the construction of various parts at makers' works is well advanced. It is hoped that the first ship will be flying at the beginning of next month. Her capacity will be 360,000 cubic feet, and her full speed endurance will be between 20 and 24 hours, according to conditions.

The principle followed in the construction of ships is that detailed drawings of every part are made on the station, and are issued through the Admiralty to contractors, who complete the various items as far as possible at their works. The parts are then collected at Kingsnorth, finally inspected, and the whole ship is put together and inflated. After the necessary trials, she is passed to one of the flying stations.

This course, although extremely laborious, has been rendered necessary by the fact that at the time that approval was received to proceed with the manufacture of airships there were no firms having aeronautical experience whose resources could be spared from aeroplane construction. It was, therefore, necessary to develop a field of manufacture on entirely new grounds. The firms that have done the majority of the work up to the present include one firm of shop fitters, four firms of waterproof garment makers, and a number of other firms such as sculptors, agricultural instrument makers, etc., who have been engaged in the manufacture of small parts.

The engines used are of the standard type in common use in heavier-than-air craft. Considerable modifications are required to suit them for the altered conditions, and this has necessitated much experimental work and detailed adjustment.

The Drawing Office started with one draughtsman in January 1914, and has now increased to a total of 49 hands. The average number of prints issued per month is approximately 1,500.

In the Chemical Laboratory research is carried out on the strength of fabrics, the results of various methods of manufacture, various dopes and methods of proofing, problems relating to the manufacture of hydrogen, and various other experimental work, in addition to routine tests of materials used in the service. One of the most interesting developments of this Laboratory is the fabric petrol tank, which is now being adopted in future ships. Tanks which have been on test for periods up to 5 months will be seen.

There is a separate Experimental Shop for dealing with instruments and experiments of various natures not directly connected with any other department on the Station.

Commander Dane showing Naval gunnery expert Sir Percy Scott around the site. (RAF Museum Hendon Q\pc72-130\085)

The plant for the manufacture of hydrogen will be seen. The average monthly consumption of hydrogen is approximately 1,422,000 cubic feet.

The development of the Station has been extremely rapid, as at the beginning of the war neither of the main sheds was finished, and there were no workshops of any description on the Station. The number of hands now working on the Station is nearly 700.

This report shows the wide variety of work being carried out on the station at this time.

A less welcome visit occurred in 1917, when the Admiralty decided to send a 'business advisor' down to look over the construction side of the station's duties. Any concerns amongst the men regarding new orders in relation to a possible invasion were nothing to the upset caused by this one man! The problem stemmed from the fact that civilian workers' pay was about double that of the service ratings. The RNAS servicemen had a lot of amenities on the station which made up for the lower wages: they didn't have to pay for their accommodation or basic food and their recreational needs were generously provided for. The businessman appears to have suggested that the civilian workforce could be cut and that their work be done by service ratings without any service amenities. Not surprisingly, the civilians felt their livelihoods were being threatened and the servicemen felt they were being taken advantage of. Senior Admiralty officials came down with more 'business advisors' to try to settle things but by this time Captain Davidson, the station commander at the time, had had enough and put in for a transfer back to seagoing vessels.

DOMESTIC DUTIES

As well as the military activity the station carried out, there were a number of more mundane tasks that needed to be done in order for the station to function. Cooking, cleaning, waste disposal and laundry were all as essential as guard duty, and probably equally unwelcome tasks for those who had to undertake them, but they had to be included in the responsibilities and rotas allocated.

Most RNAS stations followed the old navy custom of individual messing. Each mess consisted of some twenty or thirty members presided over by a messman, who drew rations, supervised the preparation of meals and washing up, and was responsible for ensuring the mess room was clean. Basic rations included meat, bread, tea and sugar, which were provided free. Other foodstuffs were considered luxuries, so vegetables, tinned fruit and jam were bought on credit from the purser's store and dry canteen, and there was a small daily allowance for each man. Accounts were settled monthly. If there was a deficit, the members of the mess would have to pay a little more to cover it. If there was a surplus, the money might be divided out or held over towards the following month's expenditure. The messman was appointed by one of the station officers. Sometimes he was supervised by an elected caterer who kept the accounts, but usually the messman did the whole job himself. It was not an ideal system as an incompetent or dishonest messman could cause a great deal of discomfort and loss before he was replaced. A reasonably competent messman would generally provide a good table without undue expense, as rations were generous and of good quality. He might even show a profit.

At Kingsnorth, the station commanders had all been keen that the men should have allotments – if the messman or any of the messmates were keen gardeners, then fresh produce would be available without recourse to the purser. Inevitably the messman was the one who dealt with any complaints and there was usually one 'moaning Minnie' amongst the men. Additional problems regarding feeding the men arose near the end of 1917 when a food-economy campaign was started. Food shortages across the country began to affect both the military and civilians. This problem was compounded in 1918, when it was discovered that the newly formed Royal Air Force, to which the Kingsnorth men were automatically transferred, was not to continue on navy rations but would change to the less generous rations allocated to army personnel.

Although there were injuries and deaths caused by the dangerous nature of the work, illnesses also took their toll. In December 1918 there was a particularly virulent strain of influenza, which resulted in several fatalities. This Spanish flu attacked healthy adults between the ages of twenty and forty. It killed about 200,000 people across England and many more in the crowded military quarters across Europe. The disease hit people so fast that you could be well when you woke up in the morning and dying by nightfall.

Recreational activities have been covered in the chapter on personnel.

4

AIRSHIPS

The military potential for airships, both over land and sea, had been debated as early as 1908, when advances in wireless telegraphy enabled ship-to-ground communication, which allowed the instant transmission of information from an observer in an airship to commanders on the ground or at sea. At the outbreak of war, the Admiralty still had very few airships and the need for more, particularly for protecting the fleet from submarine threats (the low profile of the subs made them difficult to spot from a seagoing vessel), accelerated design and production. Early military airships were all designated with the prefix HMA (His Majesty's Airship) and a number. Later the prefix HMA was replaced with the class of airship – SS, SSP, SSZ, C, C★ and NS – each class having its own series of numbers.

Kingsnorth started with two operational ships, which were used on patrol, before design and production of the first SS ships took over the station.

HMA NO. 3

Designed by the Spaniard Torres Quevedo and built by the French Astra airship company, this small, non-rigid airship, with its distinctive tri-lobe gas-bag (with a capacity of just over 280,000ft³), was the first airship to be sent to Kingsnorth, early in July 1914. She was dismantled and conveyed from Farnborough in sections, then reassembled in the newly built airship shed. Here Commander Usborne took charge of her again, having commanded her since his posting to Farnborough in April 1912. After a preliminary flight in the Hoo Valley, to ascertain that everything was in working order, the airship was brought out and, despite an adverse wind, flew to Spithead to take part in the naval assemblage there. The return trip had a following wind and was accomplished in record time.

The shape of the envelope, with the two bottom lobes forming an almost flat surface, meant that the car could be slung much nearer to the envelope, making the whole ship more aerodynamic. The grouping of the three lobes

HMA *No. 3* being hauled out of her shed at Farnborough around 1913. (Fleet Air Arm 1998/173/0061)

gave stability to the airship's shape and the enclosed car protected the crew from adverse weather conditions. Propulsion was provided by two Chenu engines mounted above the car.

Lieutenant W. Hicks RN was given command of the Astra-Torres airship in August 1914. His first patrol took place on 11 August. With a greater range than the Parseval, *No. 3* flew further to the north-east, guarding the Channel approaches. After the British Expeditionary Force was safely landed, between 9 and 22 August 1914, patrols decreased and HMA *No. 3* was posted to Ostend to scout along the coast of Belgium, including a daring flight in broad daylight over Dunkirk. These reconnaissance flights, to establish the extent of the German advance, were valuable but the airship's vulnerability to fire from the ground was a disadvantage and after a week she was returned to Kingsnorth, where she carried out night flights over London to evaluate possible Zeppelin attacks. Withdrawn for a major overhaul in the summer of 1915, *No. 3*'s last flight was on 19 August, after which she was laid up and finally deleted in May 1916, replaced by more modern designs of airship.

HMA *No. 3*'s sister ship, *No. 8*, had her trial flight at Kingsnorth on 22 December 1914. Wing Commander Usborne was the pilot and decided that modifications were needed. Between February and May 1915, *No. 8* was used by Flight Commander Hicks during the time *No. 3* was deflated for a thorough overhaul. When *No. 3* re-entered service, *No. 8* was deflated and was decommissioned the following year along with her sister ship.

HMA *No. 4* at Farnborough in 1914. The number of ground crew needed to handle one of these great airships was considerable. (RAF Museum Hendon)

HMA *NO. 4*

This German-built Parseval airship was delivered to Farnborough in 1913, shortly before the war started, despite the German government's opposition. August von Parseval, who designed and built this airship, negotiated a licence agreement with Vickers before the war. The balloon had a capacity of 364,000ft³, making it somewhat larger than the Astra-Torres ships. Ordered to Kingsnorth on 23 July 1914, it arrived four days later and was fitted out with armaments and lifebelts during the following week. As soon as the wireless telegraph arrived, orders were given to deploy the vessel, which exposed the communication problems described earlier.

Once she was back on patrol, *No. 4* provided Captain Fletcher and crew with another valuable lesson when on 13 August 1914 a propeller blade broke and flew off. It narrowly missed the rigging near the envelope. Coxswain Cook and Engine Room Artificer Shaw were able to fit a new blade, spares being carried for just this eventuality. They then decided that the new propeller blade was lighter than the original so the other spare blade was fitted opposite to maintain balance. These had to be fitted in mid-air while drifting, helpless, over the Belgian coast. Fitting new blades took an hour and twenty minutes. Cook later related that the crew could see flashes from the gunfire on the Western Front. Wing Commander J.N. Fletcher remembers that they were plagued by mechanical problems with both engines and the lights.

HMA *No. 4* was also used to escort troopships carrying the British Expeditionary Force to France and was later posted to Pulham and Howden. Reconditioned by Vickers in 1915, she was decommissioned on 17 July 1917.

SUBMARINE OR SEA SCOUT (SS) CLASS

The SS airships were just over 143ft long and nearly 28ft in diameter. The hydrogen was contained in two ballonets within the external envelope, and

SS14, one of the early production models. (Fleet Air Arm Museum UN 0024/87)

had a volume of 60,000ft³. The 75hp engine enabled them to reach speeds of 50mph. The nose cap was made up of canes in fabric pockets, which met in a small aluminium cone about a foot from the airship's nose.

The speed of manufacture and simplicity of operation of these airships enabled crews to be trained very quickly, which gave them a great advantage over the German Zeppelins.

They were ideal for escorting shipping and for searching the surface of the sea for submarine periscopes and floating mines. An airship at 2,000ft could spot a submarine 50 miles away. While a submarine could spot an airship long before the airships could see them, having spotted the airship the submarine would be forced to submerge and slow down to 6 or 7 knots, enabling convoys to outrun them with ease. If the submarine was ahead of the convoy, it was difficult for them to manoeuvre into an attacking position, but if they succeeded in torpedoing a ship, the airship could radio for assistance. By late 1917, developments in echolocation and depth charges enabled the airship crews to detect and destroy submarines even when they were submerged, and it was the proud boast of the airship men that the navy never lost a ship if it was accompanied by an airship, a boast that was very nearly true.

COASTAL, COASTAL STAR AND NORTH SEA CLASSES

The Submarine Scouts were so successful on coastal patrols that the Admiralty wanted bigger and better ships, and quickly. Three further classes, 'Coastal' (C), the 'Coastal Star' (C★) and 'North Sea' (NS), were developed. Each having larger engines, envelopes and crews than the previous classes of airship, the patrol duration increased.

On 26 May 1915, the first Coastal-class airship had its trial flight. These had an envelope capacity of 170,000ft³, a four-cockpit car and a 150hp water-cooled Sunbeam engine at each end, one set up as a tractor and one a pusher. Different engines and other modifications were tried as these Coastal-class airships became the workhorses of the RNAS throughout the war. They carried bombs or depth charges and were armed with two Lewis guns, one on the car and one on a platform at the top of the envelope. The upper gun was reached through a tube that ran from the car up to the top of the envelope, containing a special ladder with steel tubing rungs. The gun mounting consisted of a cage of steel tubing kept steady and in position by wires attached with Eta patches. It was covered with a fabric fairing and the whole thing weighed 70lb. Crew also had the benefit of parachutes. There are a couple of short newsreel clips of these ships at the Imperial War Museum.

The North Sea non-rigid airship was designed for use on long-range patrols with the Grand Fleet in the North Sea. Designed and built at Kingsnorth, this was the largest non-rigid airship built for the RNAS, with an envelope capacity of 360,000ft³. Construction was approved in January 1916 and initial flight trials of the first NS-class airship took place on 1 February 1917. As the craft was intended for long journeys, the car was designed to carry a crew of ten, who would be split into two watches, enabling them to stay up for

Improved C★3 at Kingsnorth on 26 March 1918. (Fleet Air Arm Museum E 04635/0001)

NS6 at Kingsnorth with an SS airship in the background. The North Sea airships needed a much larger ground crew. (Fleet Air Arm Museum UN0024/87)

AP1 during trials at Kingsnorth early in 1916. (RAF Museum, Hendon)

several days. The car included sleeping and living accommodation and even a hotplate fitted on the exhaust to enable the crew to have hot food. The whole thing was enclosed but it must still have been fairly cramped. Nearly twenty were built between 1917 and 1919, though the last three never entered service due to the Armistice.

AP1, THE EXPERIMENTAL 'AIRSHIPLANE'

It was a long slow climb for the early fighter planes to reach the altitude of the German Zeppelins. The Kingsnorth team hoped to solve this problem by attaching a plane to an SS airship envelope with detachable cables, enabling them to cruise at altitude and be ready at attack height when the enemy was spotted. Details of this experiment and the tragic final flight that ended both the experiment and the lives of Commanders Usborne and Ireland have been included in the chapter covering experimental work at the station.

SS PUSHERS, SS ZEROS AND SS TWINS

Work also continued to improve on the early SS design and in January 1917 the first Submarine Scout Pusher (SSP) went into service. The SSP used a 70,000ft³ envelope and a Maurice Farman-type car with a rear-mounted 75hp Rolls-Royce Hawk engine, giving a top speed of 52mph. Later they used the more reliable Green engines. Only six were built, the last entering service in June 1917.

SSZ59. (Fleet Air Arm Museum E 04636/0001)

The SS Zero, developed at Capel, was superior to the SSP. The car was streamlined, strong and watertight, enabling them to do away with skids or 'bumping bags', which meant the car could descend on to land or calm water. They were fitted with Rolls-Royce 75hp Hawk water-cooled engines, which had been specially designed for non-rigid airships. A total of seventy-seven ships of this class were built and were very popular with the crews.

The last class to be designed was the SS Twin, developed at Mullion. Their two Sunbeam or Rolls-Royce engines increased their power and the envelope had a capacity of 100,000ft³, which enabled them to carry a crew of five with a top speed of 57mph and stay airborne for up to two days.

FLIGHT OF *SR1* (ITALIAN SEMI-RIGID AIRSHIP) FROM ROME TO ENGLAND, OCTOBER 1918

Near the end of the war, Kingsnorth had an unexpected visit from an Italian airship. The semi-rigid airship design was never popular in Britain and the Admiralty only purchased one. *SR1* left ground for her flight from Ciampino, Rome, to England at 4.25 a.m. on 28 October, 1918, having on board a newly trained British crew of nine and sufficient fuel for eighteen hours at full power.

Despite three months' training and trials, it was not an easy flight. The crew were too busy to sleep as they had to battle strong headwinds and rain for much of the trip. The ship had mechanical failures, including a fractured oil line that spewed hot engine oil throughout the control car. The crew worked frantically to repair this damage but it turned the control-car floor into a slippery platform resembling a skating rink. Comical though it may sound, in an undulating control car, in the air, the crew had to take great precautions to avoid anybody falling overboard. To further the discomfort on the flight, at one point the exhaust manifold fell off the midship engine above the control car, burning through on to the petrol tanks below. The red-hot manifold lay in close proximity to hundreds of gallons of high-octane aviation fuel and beneath almost half a million cubic feet of equally inflammable hydrogen. Captain Williams and Petty Officer Leach leapt up a ladder and pushed the scorching hot metal overboard, at the same time putting out glowing sparks with their hands.

The *SR1* limped into Kingsnorth on 30 October at 12.15 p.m., becoming the first aircraft of any type to complete this journey. On its arrival, it needed considerable work to deal with an oil leak in the SPA engine. By this time, Pulham had taken over as the airship experimental station so the *SR1* went on there once the oil leak had been fixed and the crew had rested, arriving at its final destination on 6 November, just four or five days before the Armistice. Within twelve months she was deleted from the fleet.

SR1 arrives in England at last. (Imperial War Museum HU_128829)

Details of practically every single airship produced in the UK during the Great War can be found in *Battlebags – British Airships of the First World War, An Illustrated History* by Ces Mowthorpe, which was published in 1995 by Sutton Publishing. It is an invaluable source for anyone wishing to discover what happened to any individual airship and contains much useful background information on the history of airships.

The Royal Naval Air Service was also developing seaplanes and aircraft carriers during this period. These exciting and historic projects took place just down the estuary from Kingsnorth at Grain Aerodrome and Seaplane Station, north of Port Victoria, where the Hundred of Hoo Railway, built in 1882, terminated. There was a lot of friendly rivalry between the two stations' airship and seaplane pilots.

5

PERSONNEL

The ranking of officers and men changed several times between 1913 and 1918 as army and navy services were merged and then split, before the new Royal Air Force was formed in 1918. This caused confusion and friction at the time. (My attempt to produce a chart clarifying this was unsuccessful.)

In March and June 1913, letters were sent listing what permanent civilian staffing was considered necessary for undertaking repairs and refits at airship stations. It was considered vital that permanent staff were used for much of the construction work, as the various tasks required people who had undergone extensive training.

Commander Masterman requested twelve men for Kingsnorth to undertake the construction of the framework and the car that would hang below the balloon. Among this number would be engine-fitters, riggers, an instrument-maker, a photographer, an armourer, a draughtsmen and someone to do envelope design and cutting out. They also listed four women to do 'envelope work' – sewing up the doped silk to make the hydrogen-tight ballonets and outer coverings. The commanding officer of HMS *Hermes* at Chatham expressed concerns regarding women being employed at Kingsnorth. Despite his concerns, women were employed at the station, not only as fabric workers but also in the drawing office and chemical laboratory, and by the end of the war there were not only civilian women but members of the newly formed Women's Royal Naval Service, immediately nicknamed Wrens.

The original complement of men expected to be posted at Kingsnorth was eight officers, twenty-six petty officers and eighty ratings, but when it was decided to make Kingsnorth the Central Air Office in October 1913, Murray Sueter estimated that the station would require about 200 officers and men. The decision to add a second airship shed in January 1914 confirmed this estimate, listing a need for twelve officers, twenty petty officers and 130 men. There was a boat crew of five who would also act as messengers, five signal staff and telephone operators, and five postmen and orderlies. A fleet paymaster and about a dozen more staff were considered necessary in March and a ship's cook was requested as a matter of urgency on 22 May.

During the next three months, the military presence was increased even further. On 4 August Wing Commander Usborne sent in the following report on personnel:

Wing Commander	N.F. Usborne	(Commanding Officer)
Flight Commander	J.N. Fletcher	
Flight Lieutenants	W.S. Hicks and A.D. Cunningham	
Flight Sub-Lieutenant	C. Wilson	
Captain	Lord Dunboyne	(Meteorological Officer)
Captain	E. Rourke R.E.	(Military Guard)
Lieutenant	H.S. Semple R.E.	(Military Guard)
Lieutenant	Morris R.E. (temp. stationed Kingsnorth while	

block-house being built)
77 Air Service ratings
48 boys and 2 Petty Officers in charge lent from Depot as handling party
Military Guard, 2 Officers and 62 NCOs and men
1 Officer and 29 men building block-house.

All Air Service ratings (including Officers) are accommodated in the Petty Officers Men's quarters the Officers quarters being abandoned at night. Petty Officers and boys lent from Depot using Messrs. Vickers' late workmen's buildings. The Military have their own tents around the aerodrome.

That is 230 men, even if you take into account that the 30 temporary staff building the blockhouse won't be there for long, and it doesn't include any of the proposed civilian staff. The numbers were increased yet again when two petty officers and forty-eight boys were lent to Kingsnorth to bring the handling party up to its required numbers in mid-September.

In October 1914, the boys lent to Kingsnorth to provide a handling party were recalled to Chatham Depot. Commander Fletcher, who had been training them, submitted a request that, as fourteen of the recalled men were now fully trained as a handling party and more than half trained as airship crew, the two ordinary seamen be transferred to Kingsnorth as air mechanics and that the twelve boys be left at Kingsnorth and their names noted for transfer to air mechanics on being rated ordinary seamen. Commander Fletcher also pointed out, 'The loss of the 36 boys will make it still more imperative for the complement of the station to be increased.'

Over the course of the war, the complement of both military and civilian personnel continued to grow. On 16 March 1917 a signal was sent to the

This is just part of a panoramic shot of the station staff, taken in December 1918, belonging to Mike Badger, who posted it on the Kent History Forum. A similar photograph is owned by Paul Prior. It is clear that more than one photograph was taken as there are differences between their respective pictures. Easiest to see is the disappearance of the girls in mob caps on the left of the second row in Mr Prior's photograph. The seven WAFs nearer the centre of the row remain in place, so the photographs were probably taken sequentially. There are similar photographs in the archives of the Imperial War Museum in London, the Fleet Air Arm Museum in Somerset and two at the RAF Museum, Hendon.

Admiral Superintendant: 'Additional draughtsmen required at Kingsnorth Naval Air Station.' As an added incentive, the candidates were eligible for airship flying and a special bonus. The drawing-office staff were photographed in December 1918. With the Station Commander, there were another six uniformed men, twenty-four male civilians (four of these are young lads) and a dozen women. The photograph can be seen at the RAF Museum Archive, Hendon.

Examination of a scan of the station staff photo shows 618 RAF men in a variety of uniforms, including eighty-three seated at the front, presumably officers, plus nineteen WAF and 266 civilian workers, 176 women and ninety men, making the total staff just over 900 at the end of the war.

A RECRUIT'S EXPERIENCE OF THE RNAS

It seems that the only people from Kingsnorth who recorded memoirs of their experiences were officers. However, one rating who was stationed at the rival establishment down the Medway at Grain (where the 'stick and string' aeroplanes were based), set down the details of his enlistment and time in the RNAS soon after the end of the Great War. 'The Innocent Erk' by Gilbert Holland Price, was never published but the manuscript is held in the library at the RAF Museum, Hendon. It paints a vivid picture of his initial training at Crystal Palace and the routine work undertaken by ratings. This document provides a great deal of material which gives an insight into the probable experiences of his contemporaries up the coast.

Having expressed a desire to join the Royal Naval Air Service, and been given a thorough medical examination, men from all over the country were signed up and sent off to Crystal Palace to receive their kit and initial training. On arriving at the Crystal Palace, or HMS *President II* as it was designated by the Admiralty (ships' regulations applied here), recruits entered a surreal world. Among the Victorian opulence of the Great Exhibition halls, with their slender iron pillars, statues, fountains, ornamental pools and flower beds, there nestled stores, catering facilities, sleeping quarters, washrooms, market stalls (selling necessities such as soap and toothbrushes, and luxuries such as sweets and tobacco), a writing room, a photographic studio, a cinema and a dance floor complete with military band. Beyond the exhibition halls were extensive grounds, including an island of prehistoric monsters in the lake.

On arrival, their enlistment papers were scrutinised and each recruit was informed whether he would be a simple aircraftman or an air mechanic on a higher wage. Air mechanics went through a trade test on entry and they were then classified. There were engineers, motorboat mechanics, drivers, carpenters, wireless operators, riggers and hydrogen workers. Some were chosen to work with armaments or in other specialist areas.

The first pieces of kit these raw recruits were issued with consisted of a blanket, a thin mattress and a couple of hammocks. They were shown how to lash these into a bundle resembling a giant sausage before being shown where they would sleep and how to sling it. Rails and hooks had been set up at shoulder height on the galleries and part of the ground floor for this purpose. Having been shown how to sling your hammock, you were then reliant on the kindness of earlier recruits to explain how to get into it.

On the second day, uniforms were issued along with a yellow-painted canvas kitbag in which to store everything. Those with moustaches were ordered to shave them off, although a 'full set' of beard and moustache was permitted if trimmed fairly short. Civilian clothes were parcelled up and posted home. One of the elderly lieutenants advised the men to get some big handkerchiefs and use them to tie up clothing: shirts in one, number-one (best) suit in another, and so on, to prevent their kitbags becoming a hopeless muddle. There were no lockers; valuables were kept in a 'ditty box' in the kitbag along with everything else. This does not sound very secure but anyone caught stealing was not only sent to prison but on release dismissed from the navy. This was a serious threat as the inevitable result would be that they would be drafted into the army, where conditions were much worse even if they were not sent off to the front lines.

Training commenced in earnest the following day. There was squad drill on the terrace, physical training on the football field and rifle exercises. There were some half-hearted attempts to teach the men such nautical skills as complex knot-tying, signalling and compass-reading, which might have been useful had they been going to sea but were probably of little or no use to men destined to serve on the air bases. Air mechanics, in various groups, were provided with an additional course of instruction that was aimed to bring their expertise into line with RNAS practice and requirements. Before breakfast, training started with a march round the grounds, there was parade, sometime during the morning and after the midday meal (which was the main meal of the day), then various different instructors kept the men occupied until tea time.

After tea, if they were not on picket duty or part of a working party, trainees were free to relax. Before they were allowed to 'go ashore', 'on-liberty' recruits were taken to the Royal Naval Hospital where they were tested for cerebro-spinal meningitis, where a positive test meant instant dismissal. Those passed as fit returned to Crystal Palace and were then eligible for 'shore leave'. Men had to be properly dressed before they were allowed on shore and anyone not passing inspection was sent back. The queue for the liberty boat was probably longest on payday, which occurred once a fortnight.

Crystal Palace was used for training both the Royal Naval Air Service and the Royal Naval Volunteer Reserve. The designated ship of the RNVR was HMS *Victory VI*, which had a different commander. The RNAS commander in post when Gilbert Price was there in 1917 was nicknamed 'Dizzy'. He was a temperamental man, due (if you believed the rumours) to his having been sunk in a submarine. This was the man you needed to convince if you wanted special leave for any reason. On one occasion he turned down an application from one man who wanted to get married but granted the application of the groom's best man. Another time he refused an application and the disgruntled applicant slammed the door on his way out. Dizzy called the man back and asked whether he had slammed the door deliberately because he had not been granted leave.

'Yes sir,' was the swift reply.

'Leave granted. You're the only bugger that's told the truth this morning.'

Situated on the outskirts of London, the crews at Crystal Palace were turned out on many nights for air raids as Zeppelin bombers passed overhead. For some reason, the Crystal Palace itself was never bombed. There was a lot of wild speculation on why this should be but the theory that it was a good landmark seems the least unlikely explanation. Whatever the reason, the Crystal Palace survived the war, over 125,000 men were trained there and after the war it became the first home of the Imperial War Museum, between 1920 and 1924.

Imperial War Museum galleries being set up at Crystal Palace in 1920, taken by Horace Nicholls. (Imperial War Museum Q_020536)

However, it was not around as a landmark for German pilots in the Second World War as it burned down on the night of 1 December 1936.

Basic training took three weeks, after which the recruits were given any work that could be found for them while they were waiting to be posted to an air station. The wait was usually only a few days' duration. When the postings arrived there was a kit inspection and another medical examination before the final parade, where two labels, and instructions regarding what to write on them, were issued for kitbags and hammocks. A lorry was loaded with the gear and the men marched down to the railway station, where they and their gear began the journey to their designated postings. Most of these men did no flying and many of them never left Britain.

LEARNING TO FLY

Trainee pilots for non-rigid airships were sent to one of the balloon training schools, such as the one at Roehampton Naval Training Station. There they learned the skills needed to control a free balloon, vital if their airship lost motive power. Training began with large balloons with baskets capable of carrying up to eight men. On landing, the basket would often be dragged along as the wind caught the deflating balloon and was dragged along on its side, the men tumbling together within.

The conclusion of the training involved six solo flights, half of them to be done at night. One pilot recalled being sent up with insufficient ballast. Despite following the instructors' shouted order to 'Keep valving!', the balloon shot up into the clouds, about 10,000ft above the ground. The petrified trainee could hear aeroplane engines but luckily escaped a collision, returning to earth some miles away.

OFF-DUTY – LEISURE AND RECREATION

Wing Commander Usborne's hope that with good facilities on base the staff would not wish to go off base was never realistic. Permission had to be obtained to 'go ashore' in the same formal manner as if the staff had been aboard a ship in harbour. Not only were there the local beerhouses in Hoo but Kingsnorth was near enough to Chatham (with all the entertainments you would expect in a town containing a large naval dockyard), that it was possible to get there for an evening out. Popular with the officers and men was a music hall named Barnard's Palace of Varieties. The officers would be in the boxes around the walls and other ranks on the lower deck below.

Rochester had a direct rail connection to London, and those men who were able to get a day or two on leave might go up to the city to catch a show or a concert, and Turkish baths were still fashionable.

Life on the airship station was occasionally enlivened by visits from aeroplane pilots from Eastchurch. There was a lot of rivalry between the crews of the airships and their counterparts who piloted the planes. The airship pilots made fun of the 'stick and string contraptions' flown by the aeroplane

Barnard's Palace of Varieties photographed in 1905. (Medway Archives)

pilots, who responded by saying that airships drifted about like bad smells. The airship pilots delighted in taking their rivals for a ride in an airship. Still close to the ground but rising steeply they would slow down the engines, waiting for the agonised cry of, 'Look out, you'll stall the bloody thing!'

On one occasion, the pilot of a two-seater plane was showing off and got too close to one of the hangar wind-screens at Kingsnorth. This whipped off one of its wings, resulting in a long trail of aeroplane bits, at the end of which sat two very surprised flyers in their bucket seats on the ground. They only received minor injuries, although possibly their commanding officer made up for that when they returned minus their aircraft.

It was considered healthy for young pilots to blow off steam to relieve tension from time to time. It was not unusual for organised or spontaneous fights to get out of hand. One such is described by Captain T.B. Williams in his book *Pilot No.28*:

At one point a polite note arrived in the Gunroom, the junior officer's mess, from the seniors in the Wardroom. Would we join them at dinner on a stated date, with some kind of entertainment afterwards? We accepted, even more politely. We arrived well groomed and tried to be 'at ease'.

The Wardroom wined and dined us well and afterwards someone suggested that perhaps some exercise would be suitable, say a wrestling match between the two smallest in the room. The suggestion was received with acclaim. Pullen, one of my messmates, and I were selected as suitable material. We removed our natty Number One monkey jackets and carefully hung them over the backs of two chairs. All the winner had to do was place the loser's shoulders squarely on the floor.

We struggled and pushed and pulled until I decided I would take a rest on the floor, but face downwards. Pullen sat on my back and wore himself out trying to turn me over. Both of us had supporters who were roaring encouragement and I made a great heave, rolled Pullen over, slapped his shoulders on the floor and was proclaimed the winner.

This bout was so much appreciated that, after some further refreshment, it was decided to form teams and what more convenient than Wardroom versus Gunroom?

There was considerable sparring for position to commence with, each man looking for an opponent of about his own weight. At first some kind of rules were observed: Once a gentleman always a gentleman. Soon, however, as casualties occurred, there began a tendency for small groups or individuals to go to the help of their besieged, with no holds barred. An enormous Lieutenant Commander RN (not retired) noticed my light weight and seized me by the ankles and swung me round his head. Tired of knocking down opponents with my poor body he made one more swing and let me go, straight for a window, through which I went, taking the frame with me.

Fortunately we were on the ground floor and I was mercifully received by a large bush growing out of the concrete. I got to my feet in a towering rage and shook bits of window from my person. I wasn't going to suffer this indignity. I put my head through the broken window frame to size up the position only to be grabbed by the scruff of the neck and thrown across the room. I stayed where I fell in a corner. I had had enough – and I was not the only one. Casualties were everywhere and the heat of battle was dying out.

Two stalwarts were still seeking whom they might devour. There was a semi-casualty leaning against the swinging doors leading to the billiard room. The two looked at him; he had no right to be on his feet; so they seized the piano and pushed it at him. The piano slid on its wheels, hit the man and stopped at the swing doors, but he travelled on to seek his rest on the billiard table and the doors quietly closed!

I sneaked off to my cabin and so to bed.

Having read the reports from the men building these huts as to the problems they had getting glass on site, it is surprising that there were not repercussions mentioned after this incident. Perhaps having to put up with no glass in the window until it could be fixed was considered punishment enough.

The mess rooms were each given a letter of the alphabet rather than a number. There were about twenty rooms and military huts on the station, each containing about twenty-five ratings. Sporting competitions were frequently organised between rooms. There was an inter-room football championship at the beginning of 1918, for example. Facilities for storing valuables appear to have been similar to those at Crystal Palace and thefts did occur on the base. The men often had an idea about who the culprit might be and would endeavour to catch them. There was a humorous piece in *Flighty*, the station magazine, relating the attempts of one air mechanic, and his friend in the next bunk, to apprehend the thief who was operating in their messroom. They agreed to take turns keeping watch in their room, and on the night in question the one who was supposed to be on watch was dozing when he heard the pad of stockinged feet. Hunting for his torch, he dropped his weapon, a hobnailed boot, woke his neighbour and started to hunt for the thief. Not surprisingly, the two men, bumbling around in the dark, bumped into each other and a fight ensued as they tried to restrain each other, each convinced he had the thief in his grasp. This woke everyone in the room and the light was switched on, revealing our two would-be heroes grappling each other. Once they were disentangled, our intrepid heroes spotted someone walking down the road away from the hut and chased him down, racing down the road in just their underclothes, shouting, 'Stop!' The man helpfully stopped and enquired what the problem was that they were chasing after him as he was just going on watch, and telling them that the guard he was relieving would be wanting to get to his bed. While all this distraction was going on, the actual thief was able to pilfer a ten-shilling note from our hero's belongings, totally undetected.

For most of the war, the mess servants were men, but towards the end of the war they were replaced by women. This suggests there may have been a general increase in the number of women working on the station as the war progressed; the staff photograph has quite a large number of young women there. At the beginning of the war, women were employed in envelope production and there were a small number of highly educated women in the drawing office and chemical laboratory. Romantic attachments were probably frowned upon but certainly happened from time to time. The Christmas edition of *Flighty* reported the engagement of Corporal H.C. Bond to Miss 'Topsy' Abbots, both of Kingsnorth's transport department.

Wing Commander Usborne's idea that the base would provide suitable recreation facilities was not entirely over-optimistic. The station had a free library and a cinema – not surprisingly called the 'Kinema' – that put on two shows a week and boasted a high standard of excellence. One of the transport staff, Jack Haylon, had starred in a comedy called *How's Your Poor Wife?* before he joined the service and this must have caused some ribbing by his mates when they recognised him on screen, remembering that this was still in the era of silent movies. His stage name was Jack Edge.

KINGSNORTH FLIGHTY

The station newsletter was generally referred to as *Flighty*, and is not to be confused with the long-running magazine *Flight*.

Seven members of the station set up the newsletter and the first edition was published in April 1917. *Flighty* was published monthly and sold for the princely sum of fourpence, production costs being largely covered by advertising. A number of copies have survived and provide a contemporary view of what was going on at Kingsnorth. The drawing office apparently had its own newsletter, with the intriguing title *Draughtsman's Pie*.

A piece called 'Observations' by someone writing as 'Triplex' had some very uncomplimentary comments regarding the new RAF-issue boots and continued with an amusing paragraph or so on the varied mixture of uniforms that were prevalent shortly after the creation of the RAF, which he describes as the 'Great Turnover':

... aren't some of our fellows quaint looking creatures as a result of it? The weirdest collection of uniforms imaginable can be seen about now.

Everyone seems to have his own particular style, and is quite indignant if you point out any little irregularity in his dress.

We have outstanding characters, though. There's the dapper little fellow who goes ashore with the whangee cane, the only other of its kind seen in use on the Station being in the proud possession of Flight Sergeant 'Mac', he of the succulent weed in holder and the wielder of the baton. Then there is the captivating George of the plum-coloured boots and the mustard cap badge. And, thirdly, the ever-smiling Bosun's Mate, the only man to wear brown boots with the regulation jumper and slacks. But we are a happy lot for 'a that.

Other sources confirm that RNAS personnel were very resistant to the replacement of their blue naval uniform, of which they were very proud, for the khaki, army-style uniform that was supposed to be worn by the men of the newly formed RAF.

Having commented on the variations in uniform, Triplex then turned his pen to comment on the food. His sarcasm is understandable as the rations had been reduced from the generous naval allowance to the smaller rations allocated to the army.

Kingsnorth Flighty had a couple of other sections dedicated to gossip, 'What the Guards Hear' and 'Ward Room Whispers', which reported such snippets as, 'poor little Tango, the Landing Party mascot, has at last been exiled, much to the comfort of our civvy friends, to whom he was a grave menace!' Congratulations were sent to Wing Commander Cave-Brown-Cave and his bride, who cut their wedding cake with a sword, and there was some rather tongue-in-cheek sympathy for the Wrens who had just been vaccinated.

Reports of the musical entertainments put on by various members of the community, as well as fiction and poetic contributions, were commonly included. Cartoons full of in-jokes were clearly popular, and page headings for regular sections were creatively presented with beautifully decorated calligraphy. There were also articles about station personalities. News of people moving, and of those who had moved but were keeping in touch, was brief but clearly valued. There were also the inevitable and numerous reports of sporting events at the back of the newsletter, which included athletics, cricket, tennis, golf and boxing. Plenty of photographs illustrated these articles, which is surprising given official restrictions on photography and the cost of photo block-making.

CONCERTS AND OTHER MUSICAL ENDEAVOURS

The Kingsnorth Concert Party was formed in November 1916, when Mr Todd persuaded Chief Petty Officer Rednap to undertake its organisation.

Like many amateur productions now, there was a need for non-performing members and Harry Tanner was praised for the scenery he painted for the various productions.

The concert party not only entertained their fellows at Kingsnorth but took productions off to military hospitals in the surrounding district.

The dances that were held on the station had the interesting problem that there were very few women available to partner the men attending. Thus it was common practice for the men to dance with each other. Lucky was the man who managed to entice one of the few eligible women at the station to partner him. Between dances the company were entertained by songs and comic turns provided by the talented members of staff who could be persuaded onto the stage.

When the Reverend C.J.E. Peshall arrived on 26 May 1917, one of the first things he did was set up a choir. By January 1918 there was also a gas-plant choir.

The YMCA hut opened in July 1917 and hosted concert parties there. They were particularly proud of their stage, boasting it was the best in the district. They also provided new canteen facilities, though their primary aim was to serve the religious needs of the staff at the station and provide a comfortable place where they could read, write and talk. Religious services and meetings were held, and there was a regular Bible study class. Naval, military and civilian personnel were all encouraged to mix there.

GARDENING

There was clearly a group of keen gardeners on the station and potatoes were a popular crop. A humorous article on their growing appears in an early edition of *Flighty*. Those unmarried officers lucky enough to be billeted at Sparrow Castle had their own well-cultivated, kitchen garden and a run with chickens.

SPORT

Football, both rugby and soccer, were very popular, as was cricket. Athletics and running – long-distance cross-country, short sprints, and everything in between, including obstacle and relay races – were the basis of Kingsnorth sports meetings, which also featured tug-of-war contests.

The Kingsnorth ladies' tug-of-war team, which included Florrie Miskin (possibly another of farmer Walter Miskin's nieces), won the trophy on at least one occasion. Who their opponents were is a matter for speculation. We do know that Florrie was one of the large number of young girls employed in the fabric shop, and that one of her duties was helping weigh down landing airships, for which task she had to wear a special pair of heavy boots. Perhaps

The ladies with their trophy and rope, with one of the airship hangars in the background. Florrie Miskin is standing at the back on the left. (*Hoo Hundred in Old Picture Postcards*, published by the European Library)

the tug-of-war games were encouraged to improve the strength of their arms for this task.

Boxing was introduced in 1917. Billiards and snooker were popular, and one optimistic resident suggested turning part of the site into a golf course.

CHRISTMAS

Christmas was always celebrated in as much style as possible. Despite the army rations, Christmas 1918 was celebrated with great humour in the 'O' room. A copy of the menu and programme have survived, which list an interesting variety of food and some intriguing entertainment. Replete with turkey, ham, roast beef, potatoes, Brussels sprouts, Christmas pudding, fruit tarts, custards and jellies, cheese, biscuits, dessert and liqueurs, the party settled down to a variety concert with songs, comic monologues and a 'Novel Display of Skill with the Carving Knife' (the imagination boggles).

It is a sad footnote to life on the base that at the end of 1918, peace having been declared, another killer moved in – influenza. A number of people became seriously ill and several died, including Corporal Frederick George Polhill, the popular ship's cobbler. A benefit concert was organised in aid of his widow.

The Kingsnorth Gasbags were formed on the station in the sergeants' messrooms during January 1919. Those involved in their inception thought it would be good to meet up once a year, to reconnect with old friends and

Christmas Dinner at Kingsnorth 1916, probably in one of the petty officers' messrooms. (Fleet Air Arm Museum E04634/0001)

talk over old times. The first reunion dinner was held in November 1919, when many attendees were still at Kingsnorth. Unfortunately the tickets were priced too low and the enjoyment everyone felt at meeting up was offset by the loss made. The 1920 reunion dinner was fairly successful but by 1921 the enthusiasm of the members had diminished considerably as civilian life engaged their attention and energies. The association came close to folding, but a small number of stalwarts insisted that they could turn it round and over the course of the next twelve years their commitment and hard work was rewarded by a steady increase in numbers and enthusiasm.

In 1935, they put out a commemorative edition of *Flighty*, the station magazine, edited by H. W. Elliott.

COMMANDING OFFICERS

The following list of commanding officers is listed in chronological order.

Neville Florian USBORNE was the officer commanding the Kingsnorth facility from 1 April 1914 until his death on 21 February 1916.

Born on 27 February 1883 in Queenstown, Ireland, Usborne joined the Royal Navy as a cadet in 1897. He rose through the ranks, and after seven years on regular ships and five working with submarines and torpedoes he joined a team of naval men working with Vickers, Sons & Maxim at Barrow-in-Furness constructing HMA *No. 1*, the *Mayfly*, around 1908. 'Zealous' and 'capable' are words consistently used to describe him by his commanding

Commander Usborne. (National Archives)

officers. He was selected to captain the new airship, having been described as the 'outstanding personality in the project'. During handling and mooring trials on 24 September 1911, a strong gust of wind caught the *Mayfly* as she was being taken from the shed and her back was broken irreparably. Though there were no fatalities, the loss of a ship that had cost £35,000 to build led to the accusation that this had been a massive waste of taxpayers' money. In January 1912, the navy abandoned the attempt to construct large rigid airships and the Barrow operation was closed.

On 1 April 1912, Usborne was sent to Farnborough as Squadron Commander, Naval Airship Section, Royal Flying Corps Airship Wing. He was given the command of the Astra-Torres airship HMA *No. 3*, which he described as 'a handy little ship with three seats, dual control and a 40hp Renault engine'. Several of these small, non-rigid airships were ordered by the Admiralty, and on 24 October 1913 Commander Usborne was chosen to take Winston Churchill, the First Sea Lord, for a flight.

He married Betty Hamilton, daughter of artist and tea-planter Vereker Hamilton, on 23 February 1914 at St Margaret's, Westminster. Lieutenant Malone was the best man, and there was a guard of honour provided by the Naval Wing of the Royal Flying Corps.

On 1 April 1914, the Admiralty announced the appointment of Usborne as commander of Kingsnorth Airship Station and by mid-June he was in post and requesting facilities for the staff under his command.

On 1 July 1914, Neville Usborne was promoted to wing commander. At this time, the Naval Wing was renamed the Royal Naval Air Service. The first Director of the Air Department of the Admiralty was Captain Murray Sueter CB, and under him there were only five other wing commanders. One of Commander Usborne's first duties at the new station was to supervise the transport of the HMA *No. 3* airship from Farnborough to Kingsnorth and then to fly it over the Royal Fleet Review at Spithead on 20 July 1914. After the declaration of war, patrols were carried out over the Straits of Dover, escorting troopships taking the British Expeditionary Force to France between 9–22 August. On 28 August, HMA *No. 3*, carrying as offensive weapons four Hales grenades, left Kingsnorth at 6.30 a.m. under Usborne's command and landed at Ostend at 9.45. Here he spent a week undertaking reconnaissance work before returning to Kingsnorth. He was then involved in night flights over London, which were made to evaluate possible Zeppelin attacks and provide practice for searchlight crews.

Added to his responsibility for the station and personnel were problems with communication. His correspondence shows a man with respect for authority but not one who is easily subdued by it.

Wing Commander Usborne's experience in developing the *Mayfly* at Barrow made him an ideal choice for the development of a new small airship to counter the threat of German submarines. The qualities he had exhibited on that first project were sharpened even more by the need for speed. He had been given only a few weeks to design and test a simple airship, to facilitate easy training and quick production. Admiral Sueter had his appreciation of Commander Usborne's hard work and dedication placed on record. 'Far into the night and the early hours of the morning this scientific officer worked to make these airships a success,' he wrote. The result of this work was ready for evaluation within a fortnight, and in less than three weeks trials were complete and Admiral Fisher was demanding an initial production run of forty Submarine Scout airships. In all, 147 SS airships were constructed.

The production of a successful prototype and the overseeing of its subsequent production was only the beginning. Commander Usborne was constantly thinking of ways to improve performance and extend the range of these little airships. On 13 August 1915, Commander Usborne was appointed Inspector Commander of Airships at the Admiralty.

Having successfully designed an airship to neutralise the threat of German submarines, Wing Commander Usborne next turned his ingenuity to the problems caused by German Zeppelin attacks. In January 1915, the first Zeppelin raids were carried out and over the next twelve months 500 people were killed by them. Fixed-wing aeroplanes lacked sufficient speed and their climb rate was too slow to bring them within range for the effective use of their weapons. Usborne's solution – suspending aircraft below an airship envelope and the resulting fatal accident on 21 February 1916 – has been covered earlier in the book.

Commander Usborne was just thirty-three at the time of his death. His devotion to the development of airships was carried on by those who had worked with him. He provided such inspiration, and his leadership was so strong, that Kingsnorth continued to be a centre for experimental airship work after he was gone.

Roland Cecil Sneyd Carew HUNT was the interim commanding officer after the death of Commander Usborne.

He was born on 8 August 1880 in London and having joined the Royal Navy he attended the Royal Naval College in Portsmouth and was a sub-lieutenant undergoing instruction there in 1901. Lieutenant Roland C.S. Hunt was aboard the *Devonshire* (Atlantic Fleet) on the Navy List for December 1907 and in 1911 he was stationed in the Royal Naval Barracks in Chatham.

Hunt entered the Air Service on 11 November 1915, changing roles from being a commander in the Royal Navy to an appointment as wing commander at Kingsnorth Air Depot. He qualified as an airship pilot on 24 January 1916. While listed as the CO at Kingsnorth in February 1916 on the Navy List, Commander Hunt does not appear to have stayed long.

On 14 June 1916, Wing Commander Hunt married Thelma Reay Scott at St Luke's Church, Kensington. H.L. Woodcock (another officer from Kingsnorth) was one of the witnesses, and at the beginning of July, Commander Hunt moved on to become the CO at East Fortune. His command at this station earned him another promotion and on 3 January 1918 Hunt was promoted to wing captain.

Captain Hunt continued as a career naval officer and he appeared, with his wife, on the passenger list of the steamship MS *Sibajak*, returning to England from Lisbon in December 1934. Their home address was given as Byethorne, Corbridge, Northumberland.

He survived the Second World War and died on 5 December 1959 at his home in Devon, leaving a wife and eldest son, their younger son having died in 1940.

Clement Richard DANE –
CO 6 February 1916–13 March 1917.

The son of the Irish peer Sir Louis William Dane and Edith Norman, Clement Richard Dane was born on 14 September 1883, in Simla, Punjab, India. Returning to England, by the age of seven he was living with his paternal grandparents and his older sister in Hampshire.

He joined the Royal Navy as a career. He was made a lieutenant on 31 December 1905, was promoted to lieutenant commander on

Commander Dane at Kingsnorth. (RAF Museum Hendon)

31 December 1913 and was praised for his service aboard ship in 1914 when he was awarded a letter on vellum for his part in the sinking of four German torpedo-boat destroyers.

Commander Dane was granted his Aviator's Certificate at the Central Flying School, Upavon, on 16 December 1915, flying a Maurice Farman biplane, on the same day he entered the RNAS.

On 4 February 1916, Dane was graded as wing commander and appointed to the *President*, as an additional officer for the RNAS. He was posted to Kingsnorth two days later on 6 February and by December 1916 his engagement to Bessie Albina Coombe of St Werburgh Lodge, Hoo, was announced. Bessie was the only daughter of Dr and Mrs T. Sandby Coombe. He was granted leave to get married from 31 January to 10 February 1917. The Commander-in-Chief at The Nore reported that, 'This Officer carries out his duties as CO of Kingsnorth in a very satisfactory manner. He has exceptional ability and is recommended for promotion in due course.'

He was transferred to Chingford on 13 March 1917, flying aeroplanes, and was awarded the Order of Saint Maurice and Saint Lazarus by the President of the French Republic for distinguished service in the summer of 1917. Despite this, his new commander didn't think very highly of him and on 6 November 1917 it was decided he was of more use at sea as 'neither the training organisation or efficiency of this station has improved since he has been in command'.

On 9 December 1917, his wife had their first child, Richard Cecil Allen Dane. A second son, Norman Sandby Dane, was born on 24 January 1919. Commander Dane returned to the Royal Navy, retiring with the rank of captain on 14 September 1928. A year later, on 15 October 1929, he and his wife celebrated the arrival of their third and last child, daughter Elizabeth Katherine Dane.

Captain Dane returned to active service soon after the outbreak of the Second World War and on 12 September 1939 was given command of the armed merchant cruiser HMS *Maloja*. On 13 March 1940 the *Maloja* intercepted the German merchant ship, *La Coruna* south-east of Iceland but before they could capture her the German crew scuttled her. Captain Dane ceased to captain HMS *Maloja* on 29 April 1940. His oldest son, who had joined the Royal Inniskilling Fusiliers, was killed on 28 May 1940 near Oosttaverne.

Captain Clement Richard Dane died around 1963.

Alexander Paul DAVIDSON – CO May 1917–27 November 1919.

According to the Navy List, A.P. Davidson was commanding officer at Kingsnorth Airship Station from May 1917, although he may have actually been in post by the middle of March when Commander Dane moved on.

Captain Davidson had been in command of HMS *Cornwallis*, a man-of-war that had been involved in the landings at Gallipoli. He was posted to Kingsnorth and by May he was the station's CO. He was very quickly brought to a realisation of the dangers of working with hydrogen, as this incident shows:

> Particulars were given at an inquest on June 2nd of an explosion which occurred at an aerodrome at Hoo, Kent, Lieut. P. T. Armstrong, R. N. V. R., and Leading Mech. C. W. Harris being killed, while two other men were severely injured. When a fire broke out in the gas-holder it was found possible to discharge a considerable quantity of gas, and the leak was allowed to burn itself out. Wing-Commander Cave-Browne-Cave and Lieut. Armstrong subsequently made an examination, and satisfied themselves that at the time there was no flame on the surface of the holder, and Lieut. Armstrong continued to take precautionary measures, but about 20 minutes later the holder blew up. Capt. A. P. Davidson said the explosion must have been caused by a spark coming into contact with a mixture of hydrogen gas and air.
>
> A verdict of 'Accidental death' was returned in each case. (*Flight*, 7 June 1917, page 566)

Captain Davidson was keen on discipline but also had a reputation for being just when dealing with serious breaches of naval regulations.

When the Admiralty decided to send a 'business man' down to the station to improve efficiency, Captain Davidson requested a transfer back to a sea job. His colleagues believed he was not prepared to tolerate an outsider interfering with the smooth running of his ship, although it may be that he could see that, now the war was over, an airship station would provide very limited opportunities for advancement. However, he did not forget the officers he left behind and assisted the Chaplain and Lieutenant Commander Edwards to move on soon after he had.

In November 1919 Commander H. L. Woodcock RN and Lieutenant Colonel F. S. Pilling RAF had the task of decommissioning Kingsnorth Airship Station.

Harold Larpent WOODCOCK

H. L. Woodcock was born on 1 November 1882 in Allahabad, India, and educated at Dulwich College, London. By the age of 18, Woodcock had become an officer in the Royal Navy. On 28 July 1908 he was lieutenant on HMS *Skirmisher*, part of the Channel fleet. Four years later he was promoted to lieutenant commander. His career in the RNAS can be followed through a series of articles in *Flight* magazine and the Navy Lists.

On 22 January 1913, Lieutenant Woodcock was in charge of the engines as part of a crew training to handle the army airship *Gamma*, which flew from Farnborough to London. The crew were praised for the 'fine performance' of the airship. On the first Thursday in March, HMA *Beta* 'met with a slight accident at Ash' while being piloted by Woodcock during speed trials.

In April 1913 it seems he was promoted to flight commander and transferred to HMS *Actaeon*. On 20 September he passed his Aviator's Certificate on a Farman biplane in France, though exactly where is uncertain; the RNAS Flight Training Centre at Vendôme did not open until November 1916.

Lieutenant Commander Harold L. Woodcock is listed immediately under Commander Edward A.D. Masterman at Farnborough Airship Station in April 1914. Commander Woodcock was transferred to HMS *Pembroke*, in command of Farnborough Airship Station and HMA *No. 4* on 9 June 1914 and his promotion to squadron commander is recorded in the Navy List as 1 July 1914.

Flight magazine of 16 August 1917 reports that Wing Commander H.L. Woodcock (RNAS) had been awarded the 'Order of the Crown of Italy' by the President of the French Republic for 'distinguished services rendered during the war'.

Woodcock was married on 12 September 1918 at the Chapel Royal, Savoy, to Ethel, eldest daughter of W.T. Birch of Cape Town, South Africa.

The last record I found before Commander Woodcock comes to Kingsnorth is a report in the *London Gazette*, dated 10 October 1919, when he was one of a group of officers awarded a CBE in recognition of distinguished services rendered during the war.

After the decommissioning of Kingsnorth, he continued his career in the navy and was still on the Navy Lists as a retired officer in 1949.

Frederick Stott PILLING was the other officer charged with the joint responsibility for decommissioning Kingsnorth Airship Station.

Born on 13 April 1872 in Rochdale, Frederick Stott Pilling started work in the Lancashire cotton mills. He was elected as a member of the Institute of Mechanical Engineers in February 1899 and by 1911 he was working in Bristol as an engineer's manager. He emigrated to Canada with a fellow engineer, disembarking from the *Empress of Ireland* on 14 September 1911 en route to Vancouver. He returned to England from Boston, Massachusetts, on 12 December 1914.

The *London Gazette* reported, on 5 October 1915, that Frederick Stott Pilling had been issued with a temporary commission in the Royal Naval Volunteer Reserve, with the rank of lieutenant. He was posted to Kingsnorth on 29 September and a year later *Flight* magazine reports that he is among the temporary lieutenants in the RNVR to be promoted to temporary lieutenant commander. In February 1917, his CO at Kingsnorth requested 'for this officer to work in conjunction with Engineer Lt. Commdr. Markham RN'. In April his application to work abroad was turned down as his services could not be spared. By August 1917, Pilling was the station stores officer at Kingsnorth. At the end of September, his application for appointment as a recruiting officer of flying officers in the United States was not approved. Pilling was promoted to Commander RNVR in January 1918. When he was transferred to the newly formed RAF in April, his rank changed to lieutenant colonel.

In January 1919, a *Flight* magazine article on age restrictions in the RAF, which were brought in just after the war, reports, 'A selection board was established to consider applications' and Lieutenant Colonel F.S. Pilling was one of the five board members. Pilling travelled from Southampton to Halifax, Nova Scotia, at the end of October 1919, just before he was transferred to the RAF unemployed list.

After the war he returned to his career as a civil engineer, working for the government. He travelled frequently over the next seven years, visiting Genoa, Lisbon and Gibraltar. He kept in touch with the men he had served with at Kingsnorth and in the 1935 Commemorative edition of *Flighty* is listed as a vice-president of Kingsnorth Gasbags.

Pilling retired to Charterhouse Square, the Charterhouse, Finsbury, London, near St Bartholomew's Medical College. He died there on 5 May 1953, aged 81.

OTHER OFFICERS

All British air crews volunteered for the training, though many RNAS men were already on the Royal Navy Volunteer Reserve lists. Their enthusiasm for flying, whether they were officers piloting the airships or ratings dealing with the wireless and engineering side of the operation, ensured they worked hard to qualify and be allowed up in these exciting new craft.

Because of the complexity and change that was inevitable during this period, no one has yet produced a table of comparative ranks for the RNAS, army and navy, from its formation in 1914 to its amalgamation with the RFC to create the new RAF in 1918. There was a certain fluidity of terminology and the tendency of abbreviation compounded the problem. For example flight commanders were often referred to as 'Commander So and So', but a flight commander was on a par with a navy lieutenant, a rank considerably lower than a navy commander. Airships were much smaller vessels than the ships used by the navy, and confusion was caused when a pilot in charge of an airship might be referred to as 'Captain', despite the fact that they were well below the rank of a captain in the Royal Navy. Not surprisingly, navy commanders and captains objected to this practice.

Petty officers, midshipmen, coxswains, air mechanics, wireless operators, riggers, drivers, hydrogen workers, ratings and boys all added to the list of ranks and job titles used in reports, articles and books. A coxswain might start as a midshipman and rise to become a warrant officer, but still have the job title coxswain. When the RAF was formed, it adopted army officer ranks and a khaki uniform. However this was soon in the process of change as the new service began to create its own identity, separate from that of its original RFC and RNAS roots.

Lists of serving officers can be found at the National Archives, Kew, in the Navy List, copies of which are available at many libraries and archives, particularly those on the coast where Royal Navy bases are located. Family members have put information on the internet and aviation-history books mention others. During the last two years of the war, Kingsnorth Station published its in-house magazine *Flighty*, and surviving copies contain a wealth of information about the people working at Kingsnorth and their social lives. I have shamelessly plundered all these sources for information about the varied and fascinating people who were the lifeblood of this station. Unfortunately there is not room to record every officer who passed through the station but I have included as many as possible, who are listed in alphabetical order.

Percy Towns ARMSTRONG came down from Northumberland. He was an engineer engaged in gas-combustion research when he was recorded on the 1911 census, and this knowledge of gas seems to have led him to Kingsnorth Airship Station.

Armstrong was a lieutenant RNVR, aged 31, when he was killed on 26 May 1917, due to a fire breaking out in the gas holder at Kingsnorth.

Lionel Lidderdale ATHERTON was born on 6 May 1879 at Marden, near Devizes, Wiltshire. By the age of 21 he was a second mate in the Merchant Navy. He was promoted to first mate a year later and on 13 April 1905 achieved his Master's Certificate.

On 17 February 1914, he gained his Aviator's Certificate, and had become lieutenant RNR (acting), Kingsnorth, by May 1915.

He married Brenda Elizabeth Burt in the autumn of 1923 and by 1934 they had retired to Hove in Sussex. His wife died there and by the time of his death on 2 January 1956, age 77, he had moved to Great Yarmouth in Norfolk.

John Charles BARBARA, born on 3 March 1844 in Chelsea, chose a career in the Royal Navy before joining the RNAS. This chief petty officer, in addition to his station duties, took over the running of the Kingsnorth concert party after CPO Rednap stepped down from that responsibility.

John Augustus BARRON had two postings at Kingsnorth, first when he joined the RNAS in 1915 (17 March–26 May), and a year later (24 May–1 October 1916).

Reginald G. BARTON spent over twelve months in Gallipoli as a petty officer, where he was in charge of the machine-gun section of an armoured-car squadron. During this time he was under almost continuous shellfire.

He was posted to Kingsnorth as an acting leading mechanic and warrant officer in June 1915, and by 1917 Chief Petty Officer Barton was barrack master at the station. He was the first person to be chosen for a series of articles about station personalities in *Flighty*, and the last paragraph gives a clear picture of the kind of man he was:

> C.P.O. Barton is a man of very few words. He is stern but just, always willing to lend a sympathetic ear to any of the boys who are feeling troubled in the new atmosphere, to them, of Service conditions, and that he is the right man in the right place is amply shown by the esteem in which he is held by every Rating on the Station.

John Elliot 'Jock' BEVERIDGE was a petty officer at Kingsnorth. He was badly injured in a hydrogen-holder explosion in May 1917 but was reported to be 'well on the road to recovery' in the July edition of *Flighty*.

He was a seventeen-year-old apprentice engineer from Aberdeen when he signed up on 19 September 1916. He started in the army and on 9 March 1917 he was sent to Grove Park, appointed to the Army Service Corps in the Motor Transport section, before transferring to airship work.

George Alfred John BLUNDELL was born on 8 December 1882 in Hackney, London. He chose a career in the Royal Navy and was a petty officer by 1911. In August 1912, he was a gunner on the battleship HMS *Hindustan*. Between October 1913 and April 1914 he was under instruction at the Naval Flying School, Eastchurch, and by November he was the warrant officer at Kingsnorth. He continued in this post until April 1915 and sometime between then and October 1916 he returned to the sea as a gunner.

Ralph Sleigh BOOTH was born on 20 January 1895. Ralph Booth joined the RNAS on 17 March 1915. He is recorded on the Navy List of June 1915 as a flight sub-lieutenant at Kingsnorth, where he worked for over a year, gaining promotion to flight lieutenant before being posted to Howden for further training. On 28 April 1917, Flight Lieutenant Booth was posted to Barrow, where he was promoted to flight commander after two months and then flew in *R24* at East Fortune, serving as its second officer when they flew it back to Barrow. On 10 May 1918 Flight Commander Booth was posted to command Mullion Airship Station and was immediately promoted.

After the First World War, Booth continued to work with airships. *Flight* magazine reported that Flight Lieutenant Ralph Sleigh Booth AFC, Royal Air Force, was awarded a Bar to the Air Force Cross in recognition of conspicuous devotion to duty in circumstances of exceptional difficulty and danger. (The RNAS rank of flight commander and squadron commander with less than eight years' seniority did not carry over into the newly formed RAF, so Booth was ranked as a flight lieutenant in the new service.)

On 16 April 1925, as first officer of airship *R33*, he was the only officer on board when it broke away from the mooring mast at Pulham. The seven senior crewmen who were with him were also given awards and the eight ordinary crew members were to be given a suitably inscribed gold watch. Having pioneered 'mast mooring' in 1921, when his ship was torn from the tower at Pulham by a fierce storm, he and his skeleton crew succeeded in bringing her back after a three-day struggle. Flight Lieutenant Booth was promoted to squadron leader on 1 July the same year.

Booth was the natural choice for the command of *R100*. He flew her to Montreal and back in 1930, a flight and a ship which marked the zenith of British airship achievement.

Grounded by deafness in 1932, Wing Commander Booth turned his skills to the development of navigational instruments, where his influence was both profound and unsung. He retired shortly after the Second World War, alternating between voluntary work and advising on various airship and balloon ventures.

Ralph Sleigh Booth died on 12 September 1969 at the age of 74. He was described in his obituary as one of the best-known men in British airship history, remembered for his quietness in all his work and relationships.

Richard John Percival BRIGGS was born at the end of 1884 at Gravesend and educated at Hill Side School, Tonbridge. He married Isabel Russell Dartnell in the summer of 1909.

Briggs joined the RNAS on 30 March 1915 and by February 1916 he was a temporary lieutenant RNVR at Kingsnorth. He was recorded there in October 1916 and August 1917.

He died on 27 June 1979 in Stoke-upon-Trent.

Chetwode William Caulfield BROWNE was born on 29 September 1895. He entered the RNAS as a midshipman on 17 March 1915, and by 15 May had been promoted to acting flight sub-lieutenant. On 21 September 1915 he was posted to Kingsnorth and was confirmed in the rank of sub-lieutenant on 15 November. His record at Kingsnorth has a note made on the 20 May 1916: 'A good officer but does not take pains'.

On 14 June he moved to Scapa and became a flight lieutenant on 1 October 1916, before being posted to Longside on 18 November. He was at Kirkwall between 10 December 1916 and 30 April 1917, where he then settled for some time. While there, he received an early edition of *Flighty* and was inspired to start a similar journal/magazine there named *The Battle Bag*.

He seems to have done well at Longside as on 21 May 1917 his commanding officer notes:

> An experienced SS Pilot has done a considerable amount of flying in Coastal Airships. Possesses considerable executive ability. Is now under training for command. Although appointed to Air Service while still a Midshipman and consequently missing the courses for Sub-Lieut it is not considered that he would experience any difficulty in passing the various tests for promotion...

Browne graduated as an airship pilot at Cranwell on 22 June 1917 and the next comment from Longside on 11 July is: 'Excellent Pilot fully qualified in Coastals, has carried out a number of long patrols including several all night flights, has a lot of enthusiasm, and works well in the interests of the station.' Then something unspecified happened as a report on 1 October 1917 reads: 'G Pilot but appears to lack nerve. He is endeavouring to overcome this.' And again on 8 January 1918: 'G Airship Pilot. Is overcoming the lack of nerve, improving in all respects.' It seems he did improve as on 14 March 1918 he moved to Howden as captain of the Parseval airship *W7* on 14 March and went on to captain another Parseval, *W5*, the following month.

Frank Leonard Charmsbury BUTCHER joined the navy on 15 September 1913, transferred to the RNAS on 17 October 1915 and went to Kingsnorth for training. Described as keen and capable, he was posted away on 3 April 1915, returning for a longer period from 29 June 1916 until 15 January 1917. He was a lieutenant stationed at Pulham by the end of the war.

Joseph Leonard CARTER-CHERRY was born in Bedfordshire and became a carpenter and joiner in the building trade. He married Lilias L. Gardener in Surrey in 1909 and they were living in Norfolk by 1911 and were there when their son Leonard Peter was born. Joseph was a warrant officer at Kingsnorth in February 1916.

After the war he and his wife settled in Twickenham until their deaths in the late 1950s.

Thomas Reginald CAVE-BROWN-CAVE was the grandson of a Northampton baronet. He was born in 1885, and registered in Streatham. He was connected with the RNAS from its formation, having started his career at Farnborough in 1912. He was in charge of non-rigid airship design, construction and trials until 1918. In his memoirs of Kingsnorth, he emphasised the fact that they were working in an area where a great many new problems arose that required innovative methods and devices to solve them. He believed their success was due to the intimate association of those who designed, built, tested and flew the airships, careful discussions at all stages and a determination to keep things as simple as possible. His was a very hands-on approach, as his service record reveals that he even went into an airship envelope to witness first hand what happened to it when it was subjected to extreme pressure.

Flight magazine reported that he was mentioned in dispatches on 9 May 1918. He was appointed station commander for RAF Isle of Grain on 23 December 1919, and he was awarded a CBE for his outstanding contribution during the war.

During the spring of 1918, Wing Commander Cave-Brown-Cave married Marjorie Gwynne Wright, who worked in the engineers' drawing office at Kingsnorth. The station magazine, *Flighty*, reported that the happy couple cut their wedding cake with a sword. They subsequently had three children. (Marjorie has her own entry on p. 155.)

When Wing Commander Cave-Brown-Cave moved on to the Admiralty and the Air Ministry in 1919, he broadened his research working on rigid airships, and he was part of the NICAL Aeronautical Research Committee in the early 1920s. The Institute of Mechanical Engineering published papers for 1928 including one on 'The Machinery Installation of Airship *R101*', which he presented at their November meeting.

By 1935, he was involved in setting up the Southampton branch of the Royal Aeronautical Society and was their first chairman, organising lectures in collaboration with the Portsmouth branch of University College Southampton, where he was Professor of Engineering, having started there in 1931. Their branch history suggests he was also interested in power plants for airships. He kept in touch with his old friends from Kingsnorth and was one of the vice-presidents of the Kingsnorth Gasbags.

During the Second World War, he was put in charge of the newly formed Directorate of Camouflage until it merged with the Camouflage Training and Development Centre in 1945.

He was working at Southampton University when he developed the C-B-C heating and demisting equipment that Bristol Commercial Vehicles installed on their prototype Bristol FS buses in the early 1940s. Buses fitted with the C-B-C system are easily identified by the two radiators either side of the destination box. He published papers on theoretical and experimental work on turbulence, and on noise nuisance in aircraft.

He retired from University College Southampton in 1950. Later, on 19 November 1969, eleven days after the death of his first wife, Thomas married Elsie May Ricks. He died a week later, on 26 November 1969.

William Philip Clutterbuck CHAMBERS joined the Royal Navy as a midshipman on 15 May 1913. He entered the RNAS on 17 March 1915 and served at Folkestone, where he was captain of *SS13*, after qualifying as an airship pilot on 29 February 1916. In June 1916 he served with the army in France, was posted to Kingsnorth on 11 August 1917 and went to Longside on 28 September. He was promoted from flight lieutenant to flight commander in January 1918 but appears to have returned to navy service almost immediately.

Frank CLEARY entered the RNAS on 8 March 1916. On 18 March 1918, he arrived at Kingsnorth to captain the *C*4* airship and appears to have stayed there for the rest of the war.

Kenneth Crunden CLEAVER, born in 1895, went up to London from his home in Hove to join up in the Inns of Court Officers Training Corps on 2 November 1914. By 26 February 1915 he had moved to the RNVR and was a flight sub-lieutenant when he was posted to Kingsnorth in March 1915 for practical flying instruction. Cleaver's RNAS record states that his appointment was terminated on 17 November 1915 so he could accept an army commission, but other sources say he was promoted to second lieutenant (on probation) on 21 February 1916, and by 1 March this promotion had been confirmed. He was listed in *Flight* magazine as 'special reserve'.

He later became a schoolmaster and travelled to Thailand and Jamaica before marrying Pamela Margery Heal on 29 January 1942. He died on 3 October 1945 at the age of 50.

Ralph Alexander COCHRANE, born 24 February 1895, was the youngest son of the 1st Baron Cochrane of Cults. He joined the Royal Navy in 1908, became an airship pilot in 1915 and served at Kingsnorth several times between 1915 and 1920. *Flighty* notes he was a keen rugby footballer. His RNAS service record has a number of notes praising his ability as a pilot, so it is not surprising that by the end of the war he was awarded a permanent commission as a flight lieutenant.

In 1921 he met Trenchard, one of the men involved in the formation of the Royal Air Force, who advised him that the future lay in aeroplanes. He retrained and found fame during the Second World War when he supervised the execution of the Dambuster raids in May 1943. He ended his career with the rank of air chief marshal and a knighthood.

He died on 17 December 1977.

John Beresford COLE-HAMILTON was a naval cadet in 1911. He passed out as a midshipman on 15 September 1913, entering the RNAS on 30 May 1915. This airship pilot was at Kingsnorth between 19 October and 21 November 1916 before transferring to Luce Bay and Pulham.

At the end of the First World War, he continued in the RAF and gave distinguished service during the Second World War, ending the war with the rank of air vice-marshal. He died on 22 August 1945, just a few months after VE Day.

George Cyril COLMORE was born on 14 September 1885 in Hathern, Leicestershire. His father died when he was about five. His mother remarried and the family moved to Hampshire. At the age of 15 he was a cadet at the Thames Nautical Training Centre on HMS *Worcester* at Dartford. He gained his Royal Aero Club Aviator's Certificate at Eastchurch on 21 June 1910.

On 25 January 1911 he married Phyllis Isobel Fellowes and both the marriage record and the 1911 census list his occupation as 'Aviator'. The following year the couple visited Canada and their first son was born in Australia sometime during 1913.

He was a flight sub-lieutenant at Kingsnorth in December 1914, and when he was wounded in the leg by an overenthusiastic sentry whilst driving near Polegate on 16 April 1915 the story was printed the next day in the *Manchester Evening News*.

By October 1916, he was a flight commander in charge at Luce Bay Airship Station, having gained promotion at the end of June. He later became the commanding officer at Wormwood Scrubs and was listed there in August 1917, continuing in this post until at least January 1919. He and his wife had a second son in 1918 and they divorced in 1921. He never remarried. Colmore was a squadron commander RNAS when he was awarded his war service medals in November 1924.

He died on 23 June 1937 near Cirencester, Gloucestershire, in his early fifties.

Charles Sydney COLTSON was born in Natal in 1896 and by 1911 he was a naval cadet at the Royal Naval College on the Isle of Wight.

He transferred to the RNAS on 13 May 1915 and was posted straight to Kingsnorth. He is listed as a midshipman there during August 1915. He transferred on 27 October 1915 to serve at Mullion Airship Station. He returned to Kingsnorth on 18 September 1916 and was transferred once more on 1 January 1917. On 28 September 1917 he was one of the fourteen RNAS officers awarded the Distinguished Service Cross for services on patrol duties and submarine searching in home waters. He died on 25 November 1918 at Military Hospital Davenport aged twenty-two.

Herbert George COOK was born on 17 August 1888, attended the County Council School in Mickleham, Surrey, and on 23 May 1904 joined the Royal Navy at HMS *St Vincent* as a boy entrant (second class). Promoted to first class on 20 December 1904, he attained the rank of ordinary seaman in August 1906 and able seaman the following year. He was serving aboard HMS *Waterwitch* in 1911, that year he passed his educational examination for promotion to petty officer at a future date, and was promoted to leading seaman in November 1912.

Able Seaman Cook was transferred to the RFC (Naval Wing) in August 1912. Training commenced with rigging instruction, and at the end of the programme he qualified as an airship coxswain. By 1913, he was flying as coxswain on the airships *Beta, Gamma*, HMA *No. 2* and HMA *No. 3*. In the course of this year, he qualified as a balloon pilot. During his duties, he regularly flew under the command of airship captains Maitland, Waterlow, Hicks and Fletcher.

Soon after the formation of the RNAS, he was transferred to Kingsnorth, along with the airships and crews. He was promoted to the rank of petty officer in July and from August to September 1914 Cook was coxswain of HMA *No. 4*, the German-built Parseval, under the command of Captain J.N. Fletcher.

On one of their early patrols, he was one of the men involved in replacing a broken propeller blade, clambering out on the skids 1,500ft above the ground as dusk fell and the ship drifted over Belgium.

He later moved to Barrow with his ship and was promoted to chief petty officer (third grade) on 1 August 1915. Cook moved with HMA *No. 4* to Pulham and then on to Howden, training coxswains for rigid airships. He married Maude Clarke at Scarborough in April 1916. Promoted to warrant officer in January 1917, Cook was appointed trials coxswain of HMA *No. 9*, known locally as the *Silver Queen*. That August, Cook and the *Silver Queen* were posted to Howden. Not only did he fly in this ship but was in charge of rigging and was involved in trial flights for many of the later rigid airships, dealing with their numerous teething troubles. He was awarded a Distinguished Service Medal for patrol duties and submarine searching in home waters on 1 October 1917.

Promoted to second lieutenant at the time he transferred to the RAF, Cook was stationed at Short's Airship Works, Cardington, as coxswain for *R31*. While assisting with modifications, after the ship malfunctioned on

16 October, he was seriously injured in a fall from the top of the envelope. After his release from hospital, he was retained on the active list because of his extensive knowledge and experience, and given light duties, which involved him moving around, closing down airship stations that were redundant now the Armistice had been signed. He ended up at Pulham, which was being retained for experimental work of all kinds, including work on mooring masts. This work led him to oversee the building of masts at Cardington, and Ismailia in Egypt in 1927. He returned to Cardington as tower officer.

Throughout the 1920s, Cook had been in and out of hospital, suffering from a duodenal ulcer, and he was in hospital when *R101* departed from Cardington and subsequently crashed on 4 October 1930. He retired to north Yorkshire in 1932 and died there on 14 January 1970.

Archibald CORBETT WILSON was born on 21 April 1885 in Portsmouth. He grew up at Wymering near Cosham, attended the local grammar school to the age of 16 and then followed his father into the navy.

Archibald joined the RNAS as a probationary sub-lieutenant in the Royal Naval Reserve based at Farnborough Airship Station in April 1914. Within a year he was a flight lieutenant on overseeing duties. He was promoted to the rank of flight commander on 25 June 1915 and on 14 October married Lucy Ratliff. By October 1916 he was based at Cranwell Central Depot and Training Establishment. After that, he became the commanding officer at Wormwood Scrubs until 22 March 1917, when he was promoted to CO for Anglesey. This move did not turn out well and after seven months he was demoted to 'experimental duties' at Kingsnorth. The two officers overseeing his work at Anglesey recorded their extreme displeasure at 'the slackness with which he managed this station'. Perhaps the birth of his son on 12 June 1917 was the cause of this lapse.

His post-war occupation has not come to light, but it would appear that his wife died in 1963. He retired to Chichester and in 1968, at the age of 84, he remarried, to Hope Violet Brewis. He died the following year.

John Robert CROUCH became a temporary flight sub-lieutenant on 7 November 1915 and was at Kingsnorth by February 1916. He then moved to Howden and was based there until at least August 1917.

Raleigh Rosdew CUMMINGS was born at Dulwich on 4 January 1870, gained an MA at St John's College, Cambridge, specialising in physics, and spent three years teaching before undertaking a career in the Royal Navy in 1896. He was a naval instructor at Greenwich for several years and was listed as a qualified French translator for much of his career.

He married Gwendoline Vail of Halifax, Nova Scotia, in around 1910 and in 1914 they returned to Canada for a visit. Gwen died in Croydon, Surrey, in 1922.

He was at Kingsnorth between February and October 1916, and had transferred to Crystal Palace by the following August. He remained in the navy and his last posting was aboard the battleship *Queen Elizabeth* from 1923 until 1926. He was still on the Navy List as an instructor captain until his death in 1927.

Alexander Duncan CUNNINGHAM was born on 18 July 1888 and by 1904 was a naval cadet. He had reached the rank of lieutenant by 1910 and this was his ranking when he was on the torpedo-boat destroyer *Grasshopper* in October 1913 until May 1914.

By November 1914 he had moved to the lighter-than-air section, where he was first officer on the Parseval airship HMA *No. 4*. He was listed as a flight lieutenant from 1 July 1914 and had arrived at Kingsnorth by April 1915.

Cunningham was promoted to squadron commander and by October 1916 was commander at Capel Airship Station, before being posted to Barrow under the command of Wing Captain Masterman in 1917. He transferred to the RAF on its formation and married Hilda Carter in Eastbourne during the autumn of 1918. Between the wars, they lived at Stanmore, Harrow.

He died in Exeter in 1981.

James William Ogilvy DALGLEISH was born in Hove on 20 March 1888. Both his father and grandfather had been career navy officers. He was following in their footstep by 1905, and was a lieutenant aboard HMS *Cadmus* in 1911.

He was posted from the torpedo-boat destroyer *Lyra* to Kingsnorth on 1 August 1914, with the rank of flight lieutenant. James was an acting flight commander in 1915 and was the commander of the airship involved in the death of William Standford in the spring of that year, his efforts to lower the ship quickly being unsuccessful.

In May 1916, his engagement to Sybil Guinevere Butler Kennedy was announced. They married the following month, and he and Sybil subsequently had two daughters. By October 1916 he had been posted to East Fortune. On 31 December he was promoted to acting squadron commander and by the following summer was at the Air Department.

In June 1919, Lieutenant Colonel Dalgleish was awarded an OBE. Restored to the active list, he served in the RAF during the Second World War and in 1943 Wing Commander Dalgleish was High Sheriff of Rutland. After the war he wrote a book about the Rutland Home Guard.

He died in Newbury in 1969.

Francis Robert Edward DAVIS was born on 21 March 1887 and educated at St Mark's College, Chelsea. Francis married Kitty Smith in 1908 and was a fellow of the Royal Institution of Chartered Surveyors.

From 29 July 1914 to 14 December 1916 he was a lieutenant based at Kingsnorth and Pembroke. On 28 November 1917 he was attached to the US Naval Airship Squadron and was sent to New York in April 1918.

Francis was specially recommended for promotion for his pivotal role in improving the Naval Airship Squadron of the US. He was awarded the OBE in 1919 and passed the bar examination later the same year. After the First World War, he became a member of Kensington Royal Borough Council. In 1935 he was secretary of the Great Western Railway Company and was involved in organising their centenary celebrations. However, he kept up his connection with the navy. He was a lieutenant commander in the Royal Naval Volunteer Reserve and district officer of the Admiralty Sea Cadet Corps, and would later receive a CBE in 1936.

Major Davis was the commanding officer of the Kensington Sea Cadet Unit in 1942, and when he died on 12 July 1960, aged 73, he was living at 37 Porchester Gate, London, W2.

Victor Edward DEAN was born on 3 June 1897. He was a sub-lieutenant RNVR at Kingsnorth in February 1916, and the following year was one of the flight lieutenants aboard HMS *Ark Royal*. In 1918 he transferred to the RAF. He died in Brighton on 2 December 1956.

Cecil William DICKINSON was born on 5 March 1892 in Islington. His father was a solicitor and by 1901 the family had moved to Whitehaven in Cumberland to be near his mother's family. By the time the census of 1911 was taken, he had left home and was working as a marine engineer at Barrow-in-Furness.

On 27 October 1914 he joined the RNAS and went straight to Kingsnorth. He was promoted to flight lieutenant on 26 May 1915 and by January 1916 he had flown 181 hours in SS and Coastal airships. His commanding officer described him as, 'Most painstaking and keen with ability above the average' on 20 May 1916.

In June 1916, he was captain of the *C8* airship when it crashed into the sea on its way to Mullion. Of the four crew members, only the W/T operator survived. The other three crew, including Dickinson, drowned and the cause of the crash was never discovered. He was just 24 years old.

John Francis DIXON was born on 11 February 1891 and by February 1916 was a flight sub-lieutenant at Kingsnorth.

Flight Lieutenant Dixon was posted to Pulham and on 28 September 1917 he was one of the fourteen RNAS officers awarded the Distinguished Service Cross for services on patrol duties and submarine searching in home waters. He transferred to the RAF in 1918.

David S. DONN joined the RNAS on 17 March 1915. His CO dismissed him as 'Somewhat dense but tries hard'. He was still a midshipman at Kingsnorth in February 1916, leaving to go to Longside. At the new station, his new CO had a very different view of this officer: 'Keen efficient Officer, very experienced pilot with good organisational ability'.

Kinsley Dryden DOYLE was born in Dublin on 10 April 1864. Before the First World War he was a civil engineer and worked in both North America and South America.

He was at Kingsnorth by October 1916 and was the lieutenant in charge of the armament department there in 1918.

After the war he settled in Willesden with his wife Mary Susanna, and died there during the summer of 1928.

Hedley Vicars DREW was born on 13 January 1897 in Oxford. Hedley was one of the many midshipman 'loaned' to the RNAS on 13 May 1915 and he was officially posted to Kingsnorth in August 1915. Having been trained at Kingsnorth, he went on to Barrow, where he was promoted to flight sub-lieutenant in March 1916. From Barrow he was posted to East Fortune and by the end of 1916 had been promoted again, becoming a flight lieutenant. The senior officers at East Fortune thought Flight Lieutenant Drew had potential and he was sent to Cranwell on 7 February 1917, where he graduated as an airship pilot, qualifying as a 'Coastal' pilot in June of the same year. On 25 October 1917 he was moved to Pulham where he was working as second officer on *R23*. His final promotion was to temporary captain on 17 May 1918.

After the war, Flight Lieutenant Drew continued to work with airships. He was captain of the *R34* when it was being test-flown, after a major overhaul and a period of inactivity, on 27 January 1921 from Howden. That evening, the weather turned bad off the Yorkshire/Durham coast, visibility was reduced and the airship drifted inland. In the early hours of the next morning, a sudden downdraft caused the airship to strike a glancing blow on high ground south of Guiseborough. The ship bounced off the moor and back into the air, waking the off-duty crewmen in their bunks. Captain Drew ordered the engines stopped while the damage was inspected. The front gondola had been badly smashed and had heather stuck in its engine, making it useless, and the aft car had lost its propellers. A distress signal was sent and

HMS *Wrestler* and HMS *Walker* were ordered to stand by in case *R34* drifted out to sea, and a tug stood by on the Humber in case it ditched there. Luckily these precautions were not needed as Captain Drew and his men were able to get the ship back to Howden using the engines on the wing cars, though it took them fifteen hours. Back at Howden, high winds then prevented the ground crew getting it into a hangar and after struggling with it for another hour and a half, they eventually managed to moor it to some trees in a nearby field. On inspection the following day, it was found to be too badly damaged to be repaired and over the next three days it was scrapped.

Drew died in Chichester, West Sussex, towards the end of 1977.

Thomas Ronald Hilliard DUFF was born in Worcestershire in September 1890. His father had been born in India and the family moved around a lot before settling in Fife. Duff joined the RNAS as a flight sub-lieutenant on 17 December 1914. Having trained at Wormwood Scrubs, he was posted to Kingsnorth on 15 March 1915, as second officer to HMA *No. 3* and in October was sent on courses covering engineering and Sunbeam and Rolls-Royce engines.

He gained promotion to flight lieutenant in April 1916 and promptly left England for the Eastern Mediterranean in the P&O vessel SS *Kashmir*. In November 1916 he was at Mudros, where he completed works on the repair base and workshops, returning to England just in time for Christmas. Duff was posted to Capel on 27 February 1917, after two months' leave. In October he was posted to the *R14* section of the Air Department to work with Wing Commander Maitland and was recommended for promotion in December. His CO remarked that he was hard-working and conscientious and at the end of January 1918 he was promoted to acting flight commander.

Around the beginning of 1916 he married Dorothy Lovelace Wagon by special licence. They had no children and divorced before she died in 1941. He died in Surrey early in 1960.

S.L. DUFF was a sub-lieutenant posted to Kingsnorth in August of 1915.

Lord DUNBOYNE was born 20 March 1874. Dunboyne fought in the Vitu Expedition in 1890. He succeeded to the title of 17th Baron Dunboyne, County Meath, in August 1913 and retired. However his retirement was short-lived as on 3 November Captain Dunboyne was back, undertaking meteorological duties on the books of HMS *Hermes*. His work as a meteorological officer at Kingsnorth continued throughout the First World War.

On 26 July 1915, he married Isolde Butler Tower, with whom he had a son and three daughters. He died on 9 May 1945.

P. Harrington EDWARDS joined the London RNVR with the rank of sub-lieutenant in September 1914. After training, his first posting was Gallipoli, where he was seriously wounded. On his recovery, he returned to action and was again wounded. During this campaign he was promoted, first to lieutenant and then lieutenant colonel after the evacuation of Gallipoli, when he was the last officer to leave his sector of the front line. He had a narrow escape when HMS *Hythe* was rammed by another vessel, jumping across at the moment of impact. He was in temporary command of the Howe battalion at Stavros and Salonica, before being posted to France. Here Edwards was placed in charge of the main firing line until, on 13 November 1916, at the Battle of the Ancre, he was seriously wounded in four places and lost his left eye. He recovered but was no longer allowed to fight on land. He was in charge of troops on board HMS *Leasowe Castle* when it was torpedoed, but it was not until he contracted rheumatic fever at Gibraltar that he was finally returned to England.

It was then that, having informed his superiors that he was a founding member of the Royal Aero Club, Edwards was appointed executive officer at Kingsnorth Air Station. Like many before him, he arrived at Ashford, the nearest station to Kingsnorth village, and asked the bemused local cabbie to take him to the aerodrome. On arrival at the airship station, he discovered he would be taking over from Lieutenant Commander Mackenzie and that his extensive duties had little to do with flying. He was, according to his RNVR records, too young to be promoted to the position of commander, but it was discovered he had lied about his age when he joined up and was in fact eligible for promotion to that rank. He served under Captain A.P. Davidson, who arranged for Edwards to return to navy service aboard HMS *Hindustan* and whose confidence in him prompted a recommendation that the commander be appointed as the intelligence officer when the expedition to the Zeebrugge mole was being organised for 23 April 1918.

Edwards became second in command to Captain Halahan, the officer in charge of the naval storming parties aboard HMS *Vindictive*. The ship was under constant heavy fire, Halahan was killed and Edwards badly wounded in both legs before they could lead the men ashore. Commander Edwards went on to be executive officer of HMS *Glory IV* and on arriving at Archangel in northern Russia recruited and commanded a special brigade, the Russian Allied Naval Brigade.

In 1935, Commander P. Harrington Edwards was the president of the Kingsnorth Gasbags, a group of former Kingsnorth personnel who had kept in contact since the end of the war and the decommissioning of the station.

Thomas Walker ELMHIRST was born in December 1895. He joined the RNAS on 17 March 1915, trained at Kingsnorth until 2 April and then served at Luce Bay and Howden.

Elmhirst continued his career, serving in the RAF, reaching the rank of air marshal. He returned from Malta with his wife Katherine and baby daughter in 1932, was knighted, and in 1939 returned from India where he had served as commander-in-chief of the Royal Indian Air Force.

He lived with his wife in Fife after he retired. After Katherine died in 1965, he returned south and remarried, to Marian L. Ferguson. He died in Dummer, near Basingstoke, towards the end of 1982.

John Pascoe ELSDEN was born in Staines on 9 May 1887. In the 1911 census he and his new bride, Violet Mary, are listed as staying at a hotel in Brighton. Elsden was a barrister by profession. He worked in the anti-aircraft service before entering the RNAS on 3 June 1915, as a sub-lieutenant in the kite balloon section temporarily before being attached to the Board of Invention and Research for experiments and investigations. While there, he was not paid by the navy but from funds allocated to the Board by the Treasury. In December 1915 he was promoted to lieutenant and undertook armament duties at White City before being transferred to Kingsnorth on 7 February 1916. 'Pascoe' was lent to the Air Department for temporary duty with the captain responsible for armaments on 22 July, and on 5 August he was transferred to the Air Department 'G' section. In October 1917 he was lent for duty with the deputy controller of armament construction. Around this time, he applied for permission to serve at sea. His request was refused as his services were deemed indispensable, but he was recommended for promotion and on 1 January 1918 he advanced to the rank of lieutenant commander.

After the war he returned to the law and in 1920 he and his wife went to live in the Caribbean for a year.

He died in the spring of 1950.

Albert Victor FAULKS was born in London around 1886, and before the war was a chartered accountant. Sub-Lieutenant Faulks was the fleet paymaster's assistant at the station, from around October 1916 to at least August 1917. He did a lot of clerical work for the station captain. By 1919 he was an acting paymaster lieutenant, registered on the books of HMS *President*. At this time few stations had their own dedicated paymaster and he was probably responsible for payments on a number of air establishments.

He retired to Scotland and died there on 26 January 1956.

John Norman FLETCHER, born on 19 March 1889, attended Berkhamsted School. He joined the navy as a clerk in 1900 and by 1911 was in the Royal Engineers, based at Chatham. Lieutenant Fletcher gained his Aviator's

Certificate on 8 June 1912 in a Cody biplane and a month later he received his Aeronaut's Certificate and his Airship Pilot's Certificate. In 1913, he was captain of the army dirigible *Gamma*, which he landed in the grounds of his old school at Berkhamsted Castle. In July 1914 he was published as the co-author of an article on 'The Value of Ballooning as a Training for Flying' in *The Aeronautical Journal* 18, no. 71, and in September the same year he was quoted in the *New York Times* regarding the use of airships for night bombing raids.

On 23 July 1914 the Parseval airship HMA *No. 4* arrived at Kingsnorth and Lieutenant Fletcher was given command of this German-built craft. He was the first captain to be sent out on patrol from Kingsnorth and his first flight showed up problems in communication procedures. During his time as captain of the Parseval airship, he dealt with broken propeller blades and problems with both the engines and the lights.

Fletcher was only at Kingsnorth for three or four months before he was given the job of forming the RNAS Photo Section. Having set this department up, Fletcher was then sent to Barrow to supervise the construction of two airships being built there by Vickers. In 1916 Fletcher was appointed to the Admiralty Air Department for a brief spell before being transferred to Cranwell. He went on to Longside, returning to Cranwell in 1917, where he experimented with parachutes. Fletcher rose to the rank of wing commander and in March 1918 was lecturing at Cranwell on the constructional methods of airships and balloons. From there he moved to Inter-Allied Aeronautical Commission of Control (Hungary), and on 14 November 1921 he was transferred again to the Air Ministry for stores staff duties.

Little is known of J.N. Fletcher's career beyond his involvement in this intensive programme of airship development. In 1982 Blandford Press published the book *Airship Saga* and Wing Commander Fletcher contributed his memories of the early days of British airships.

He died in Surrey on 27 December the following year, aged 94.

Ivor FRASER was born on 18 January 1881. He transferred from RNVR Armoured Cars in Barrow to the Naval Air Service on 15 September 1915. In January 1916 he was sent to Wormwood Scrubs and returned to Barrow on 2 February having completed his balloon training. On 23 March he was posted to Howden and a couple of weeks later was en route for the Mediterranean, serving first at Kassandra Airship Station and then at Mudros.

On 8 September 1916, injuries to his left knee prompted the Admiralty to propose he be sent to Kingsnorth. His promotion to flight commander arrived at the end of 1916, the day before he was due to start at Kingsnorth.

A fortnight later he was transferred to Polegate and on 5 February 1917 he put in for appointment as commodore, Crystal Palace. On 26 April he was granted three weeks' sick leave, returning to Polegate on 19 May. He was recommended for promotion on 12 October and at the end of the year was awarded the rank of squadron commander. The wing commander for the Portsmouth group recorded that the RNAS Polegate, under the command of Flight Commander Ivor Fraser, had carried out a very large number of patrols, considerably more than any other airship station in the RNAS, in both the number of patrols carried out and the mileage flown during the period since it had been placed as part of his group.

Hugh Clarence FULLER was a flight lieutenant, Special Services, Kingsnorth, in December 1914. He returned to Kingsnorth for three months from 4 September 1917, leaving to become officer in charge of Marquise Air Station on 6 December. He returned again to Kingsnorth on 4 January 1918 to command NS5 and later NS7, having been demoted from his post at Marquise, where his fining of officers for breaking leave was considered 'perilously near to a gross irregularity'.

F.W. GARDNER became a temporary lieutenant RNVR on 12 March 1915, was stationed at Kingsnorth by February 1916 and stayed there until 1919, when it was in the process of being decommissioned. Gardner had risen to the rank of lieutenant commander by August 1917 and in 1919 was a major in the newly formed RAF.

Robert Victor GODDARD was born 6 February 1897. Goddard was a naval cadet before he joined the RNAS on 13 May 1915. After initial training at Roehampton and Hurlingham, Midshipman Goddard arrived at Kingsnorth for further training in June 1915, which included aerostatics, meteorology, theory of gases, design of non-rigid airships, permeability of fabrics, fabric dopes, rubber adhesives, structures, wire splicing and airship instruments (he was able to skip navigation as he had learned this in the navy earlier). Each pilot supervised the construction of his own airship so he knew every inch of it and understood exactly how it worked.

All the training was completed before he was posted to Barrow-in-Furness the following month. From Barrow he moved to Capel-le-Ferne for four months, spent a month at Polegate and was then attached to the RFC at Boubers-sur-Canche, where he was involved in experiments with dropping agents behind enemy lines.

Goddard returned to Kingsnorth for a spell from December 1916 to March 1917. He then moved to Pulham, where Wheelwright and Maitland were experimenting with parachutes. After about a month of ground work in August 1917, Goddard moved on to East Fortune, during which time he visited Kingsnorth to collect and fly back *NS5*. He continued to move around, serving on HMS *Indomitable*, where he was involved in experiments taking off from a platform on the ship. At Pulham he experimented with mooring at sea, and then moved on to Walney Island, supervising the assembly of *R80* and preparing to fly *R34* across the Atlantic.

He studied engineering at Jesus College, Cambridge, and worked at the Royal Naval Staff College between the wars. During the Second World War he served in the RAF, was awarded a CBE in 1940, rose to the rank of air commodore and was appointed chief of New Zealand Air Staff in 1941. He visited Canada in September 1942 and in 1943 was put in charge of the administration of the South East Asia Command. In 1946 he was the RAF representative in Washington and was knighted in 1947. He retired in 1951.

Goddard recorded his varied and fascinating experiences during his time working on airships in an interview at the Imperial War Museum in 1973. He died on 21 January 1987.

C.H.W. GODFREY was a flight sub-lieutenant at Kingsnorth in February 1916. By August 1917 he had been promoted to flight lieutenant and moved to Pulham.

Alfred Sebastian GOODWIN was born on 7 October 1877 in Hampstead. His father was Professor of Greek at University College London. By the age of 23 Alfred's father had died and he was working as a civil engineer. In 1911 he was still single, living with his younger brother Aubrey, who was a medical student, and a housekeeper.

His service record shows that he joined the RNAS on 29 April 1915 but did not become an officer until 5 August 1915. He is listed on the books of HMS *President* from 29 April 1915, later transferred to Barrow and was an engineering officer at Luce Bay on 14 May 1915. His elevation to acting flight lieutenant on 5 August 1915 is the promotion that places him in the officers' records, and it was also the date he passed his Aviator's Certificate at Hendon. Goodwin's commanding officer at Luce Bay clearly thought highly of him, as on Boxing Day 1915 he recommended confirmation of his rank as a flight lieutenant. Despite describing him as thoroughly reliable and an excellent officer in every way, capable of command, the application for his rank to be confirmed was not approved. This may have been because of the damage he did to a BE2c biplane during a forced landing north of Scarborough Aerodrome, though the plane was not seriously damaged and he was uninjured.

In March 1916 he was again described as a thoroughly reliable and efficient engineering officer but at the beginning of June he was again denied confirmation in the rank of flight lieutenant. At the end of June 1916 his

CO tried again to recommend his rank be confirmed but this still had not happened by the time he was transferred to Kingsnorth on 20 September.

At Kingsnorth, he again impressed his CO and although he failed to graduate as an airship pilot at Wormwood Scrubs on 21 September 1916, he passed in buzzer semaphore, flag Morse, aerial navigation and map-reading at Kingsnorth on 16 October. Three days later the CO at Kingsnorth received the suggestion that Goodwin should not be confirmed in the rank of flight lieutenant until he had passed the graduation examination. He graduated as an airship pilot at Kingsnorth on 30 October 1916 and on 7 November was posted to East Fortune, where his commanding officer described him as hardworking and zealous.

On 21 May 1917 Goodwin was posted to South Shields, where he again impressed his CO, who noted that he was 'excellent in charge of artisan ratings, has wide experience in many branches of engineering'. The CO considered him deserving of promotion and recommended him for the rank of flight commander.

In July 1918 he joined the Technical Branch of the Royal Air Force, and was finally granted a short-service commission as a flight lieutenant on 9 July 1920, serving in India around 1922. In July the following year he transferred to the Reserve list and finally relinquished his commission on the grounds of ill health on 22 September 1926.

During the last quarter of 1927, he married Beatrice Plympton Clayton. They had at least one child before he died aged sixty-eight, in the late summer of 1945, registered in Marylebone.

Henry D. GRAHAM joined the navy as a boy and by the age of 14 was a cadet at the Royal Naval College on the Isle of Wight. Posted to Kingsnorth on 17 March 1915, he was listed as a midshipman there in August 1915. He was transferred on 22 September 1915 and served in the eastern Mediterranean.

F.W. HAMMOND was a fleet paymaster, posted to Kingsnorth around August 1915 and still there in August 1917. After the war he continued as a paymaster in the Royal Navy.

Douglas HARRIES was born on 31 March 1893 in Sidcup, Kent, and entered the RNAS on 18 December 1914. By 1 April 1915 he was a flight lieutenant and had just been stationed at Polegate. On 1 January 1916 a remark is entered on his record from Dover stating that he was, 'very good in airships and his Station is in order, he is rather lacking in experience as regards disciplinary matters but is improving'. He had flown over 100 hours at this point and it was expected that he would make an exceptional officer.

Flight Lieutenant Harries was transferred to Kingsnorth on 4 March 1916 and he was the official photographer there in April. During the spring of 1916 his commanding officer at Kingsnorth recommended him for promotion three times. He was promoted to flight commander on 30 June 1916. A year later, having qualified as a pilot of Coastal airships, he had been promoted again, to the rank of squadron commander, and was the senior flying officer at the station. He got a full-page photo in the station magazine *Flighty*. His CO at Kingsnorth described him as having exceptional ability and power of command just before he was posted to Barrow in July 1917, where he impressed them as being a very capable officer.

Harries continued his career in the Royal Air Force after the war. He was also a first-class cricketer, playing for the RAF in 1919 and the Free Foresters team between 1919 and 1920 against Oxford and Cambridge University teams. In 1938 he and his wife Stasia returned from Australia to their home in Willingdon, Sussex, having been stationed in Trans-Jordan.

Douglas Harries died on 6 December 1972 at Crondall in Hampshire. He was nearly 80.

Douglas HARRIS was a flight lieutenant listed at Kingsnorth in May 1915.

Irving Henry Bebby HARTFORD was born in Christchurch, Hampshire, on 30 May 1890, the eldest son of a surgeon. On 5 August 1910 he was awarded a certificate of competency as second mate for foreign-going steamships. He was probably working on ships which travelled to India, as when he joined the RNAS on 7 September 1914 he listed with an ability to speak Hindustani.

Hartford trained at Farnborough and was a flight sub-lieutenant at Kingsnorth when he became a flight lieutenant on 31 December 1914. In January 1915 he went to Dunkirk and in February was attached to HMS *Manica*, transferring again in June to HMS *Hector*. In March 1916 he was diagnosed with neurasthenia, now commonly called chronic fatigue syndrome, and spent nearly three months on sick leave, returning to duty at the end of May. His sickness did not prevent his promotion on 30 June to flight commander while he was at Roehampton. He attended a short course at Kingsnorth in July before being posted as a temporary commanding officer at Anglesey Airship Station. He returned to Kingsnorth briefly in October and was then appointed commanding officer at Luce Bay.

Throughout 1917, his commanding officers describe him as 'in command, thoroughly reliable and efficient', and he was recommended for promotion. He was mentioned for good service in August and the following month received a commendation for his conduct and handling of *SSZ13* under difficult circumstances during a night flight. On 31 December 1917 he was promoted to squadron commander. In April 1918 he was posted to East Fortune to captain *R24* and two months later he and his ship moved to Howden. In January 1919 he was stationed at Pulham.

In the spring of 1919 he married Dorothea E. Hartford at Headington, near Oxford. After the war he joined the Marines and on 29 September 1935 he was on his way to Mexico, where he intended living. Dorothea was not with him.

In 1946 he was on the electoral register in Kensington but by 1948 he had moved to Camden. He died around March 1980 in Southampton.

Hamilton HARTRIDGE was born on 7 May 1886 at Stamford Hill, London. His father was a wool importer, but in his spare time he was a skilled cabinet-maker and had the mechanical aptitude to mend most things, including clocks and bicycles. His uncle was an engineer and both encouraged him to take an interest in science. At Saint Vincent's Preparatory School, Eastbourne, Hamilton was taught carpentry by 'a pleasant old boy, an ex-seaman'. He was also interested in photography and when he went to Harrow his mechanical inventiveness developed in leaps and bounds. Hamilton studied medicine at King's College, Cambridge, and when he obtained his fellowship in 1912 his grandmother gave him a car. He promptly drove to visit his cousin Kathleen Adele Wilson, near Derby, and took her out. They became engaged in 1913. Hamilton qualified as a doctor in 1914. By this time he had already become well known as an inventor and when he joined up in 1915 he was sent to Kingsnorth Airship Station as a problem-solver. His post as experimental officer suited him and Lieutenant Hartridge was soon engrossed in providing rapid solutions to the new and unexpected problems thrown up by the science of air warfare.

He and Kathleen married in 1916. They had four children. After the war, Hamilton returned to King's College and became a Senior Demonstrator of Physiology and a Lecturer on Special Senses. His lectures and practical classes were noted for being experimentally orientated. He published about seventy papers during his time at Cambridge. In 1927 he moved to St. Bartholomew's Hospital Medical School as Professor of Physiology.

He became the first director of the newly established Institute of Ophthalmology in 1947.

Retiring aged 65, he enjoyed another fourteen years in retirement before his death on 13 January 1976.

Charles J. W. HATCHER was a coxswain at Kingsnorth in the early days. His experience in airship construction and rigging, and his work as part of the erection party on North Sea airships, all counted towards him being gazetted as a probationary flight officer in the early summer of 1917.

C.N. HAVENS, nicknamed 'Winkle', left Kingsnorth on 9 April 1918 and was stationed briefly at Vendôme, France, before joining a squadron in Paris. This squadron was sent up the line to a well-camouflaged base, where the workshops were practically underground. Despite the camouflage, the base was discovered and blown up in October 1918. Havens was knocked out and came to on a hospital train bound for Rouen. His injuries were severe enough that he needed to be shipped back to England.

He recovered and, as he still had a year before his time in the RAF was completed, he was posted to north Russia in May 1919. While serving there he had a number of interesting and exciting experiences, including being in a small party captured by Bolshevik revolutionaries; all of them managed to escape. His service in Russia was recognised by the White Russian authorities and he was awarded the Russian Silver Medal with the ribbon of Saint Anne.

Havens was a keen supporter of the Kingsnorth Gasbags and wrote an extensive and entertaining account of his exploits as part of the North Russian Expeditionary Force for the 1935 anniversary edition of *Flighty*.

Robert Cholerton HAYES was born in Sheffield in 1884. By 1901 he was a naval cadet. The *London Gazette* of 10 April 1906 confirms him in the rank of sub-lieutenant and in 1907 he was promoted to lieutenant.

On 30 March 1915 he was promoted again, this time to the rank of lieutenant commander. He joined the RNAS on 28 February 1916 and after a spell at Wormwood Scrubs spent two months (14 April to 14 June) at Kingsnorth. He moved around a lot over the next few years, including three more brief postings at Kingsnorth. He was awarded an OBE for services during the war.

He returned to the navy and, having attained the rank of lieutenant commander, was granted a certificate of service as master of a foreign-going ship. Retiring from the navy in 1922 he later went into the Colonial Office. Despite suffering from sunstroke and recurrent malaria, he was sent to Malaysia, where he spent three years before his health broke down completely and he returned to England.

He died from ingesting poison in 1927, aged 42. Sadly, the inquest concluded that he had committed suicide while of unsound mind.

Sidney Reynolds HIBBARD was born in Gloucestershire in 1876. He was listed as a sub-lieutenant RNVR on 13 August 1914 and was stationed at Kingsnorth. In January 1915 he was promoted to flight lieutenant and moved to Grain to fly heavier-than-air craft, where his commanding officer reported that he was hard-working and conscientious.

In August 1916 Hibbard applied for service abroad and was appointed to the Handley-Page squad at Manston in October and left for France on 1 January

1917 in *HP1463*. He did not arrive at his base in France and that, coupled with a German claim to have captured a 'super aeroplane' led the RNAS to conclude he was a prisoner. By August 1917, his status as a prisoner of war was confirmed: he had been captured at Chaland and was interned at Brandenburg. Being a prisoner of war seems to have prevented his transfer to the RAF in January 1918.

Harold Edward HICKMOTT was born on 8 May 1881 in Rotherham. He married Gertrude Madeline Blight towards the end of 1909, and by 1911 he was living and working as a marine and ordnance engineering draughtsman in Cheam, Surrey. Their twin boys were born in 1913.

Hickmott joined the RNAS on 16 July 1915 and was a temporary lieutenant RNVR at Kingsnorth until February 1916. During this time he completed balloon training and an armaments course at Wormwood Scrubs. His CO considered that 'he has no power of command and does not appear likely to develop it. He would make an excellent officer in charge of stores'. By October he had been posted to Gibraltar and then moved to Eastchurch, before being stationed at Pulham in August 1917. From Pulham he moved to Milford Haven for 'G' duties.

By the 1930s he was a company director with business connections in Bermuda. He died in Devon on 19 August 1947.

William Charles HICKS from Southsea was granted his Aviator's Certificate on 27 May 1913 at Ewen Flying School, Hendon, having flown a Caudron biplane.

His promotion from flight lieutenant to flight commander was reported in *Flight* magazine on 8 January 1915 and he piloted the BE2c designed by E.T. Busk in August. Notice of his promotion to squadron commander appeared in the *London Gazette* of 28 July 1916. He carried out successful flight tests on the *AP1* airship before its fatal crash.

At the end of the First World War he joined the RAF, was promoted from wing commander to group captain in July 1931, and he died on 26 June 1939.

Sydney Robert HILL joined the RNAS as a temporary lieutenant RNVR on 5 October 1915. He was at Kingsnorth in February and October 1916. By August 1917 he had moved to the Admiralty Air Department.

William Raymond Milner HILL was a flight sub-lieutenant at Kingsnorth in February 1916.

Leonard Cyril HOOK was a warrant officer who arrived at Kingsnorth in September 1915.

Herbert Edwin HORNE was born around 1886. He was working as an insurance agent when he married and he and his wife were living near Streatham Common when he joined the RNAS on 26 July 1915. Horne served as a lieutenant RNVR at Kingsnorth until April 1916, when he was assigned to inspection duties. In August 1917 he was lent to the Ministry of Munitions and three months later was in Greenwich Hospital with a fractured right arm, after which he disappears from the service records.

William F. HORNER trained at Kingsnorth between March and 10 August 1915 before being posted to various other stations. He was at Kirkwall from 12 March 1917 and had an application to return to sea service turned down, as trained airship pilots were too valuable to let go. On 21 December 1917 he disappeared with his ship and crew and was presumed killed.

Samuel HOULT was a chief petty officer who left Kingsnorth in 1917. *Flighty*, the station magazine, reports on his departure and says:

> When he took over Office as Barrack Master he did so in trying times. That he was successful was acknowledged by all who were here, and station routine in his hands was more pleasant than that of earlier days. Sammy believed in making things as easy for everyone as discipline would allow, and his interpretation of the King's Regulations robbed them of much of their sinister aspect. During his term of office he completed his twelve years' service in the Navy which he celebrated by a riotous night with the boys. He was blessed with that rare faculty of being able to get his orders carried out sharply and to the letter without friction with either Officer or man.

He left the barrack office when he was put in charge of the erectional party.

H.R.J. HUGHES was a New Zealander attached to the maintenance department at Kingsnorth and inevitably was nicknamed 'Anzac'. For a short time he was the engineer on *SS14* before leaving around September 1917 to go on a flying course. Gaining experience in a number of machines, he became an efficient pilot and by May 1918 was engaged in long-range bombing missions overseas.

Philip Henry HUNTER was born in Brighton towards the end of 1885 and by 1911 he was a petty officer telegraphist in the Royal Navy, stationed in the Mediterranean. He was listed as a warrant officer at Kingsnorth in December 1914 and April 1915. By October 1916, Warrant Officer Hunter had moved to White City and was still there in August 1917. By January 1919 he had been posted to Dundee as a warrant telegraphist and by July 1920 he was listed in the RAF.

De Courcy Wyndor Plunkett IRELAND was born on 18 January 1885 at Merton Hall, Borrisokane, County Tipperary, Ireland, and attended Christ's Hospital School, Horsham.

On 1 November 1913, Lieutenant Ireland was awarded his Flying Certificate at the Naval Flying School, Eastchurch, flying a Bristol biplane. Flight Commander Ireland was elected to the Royal Aero Club towards the end of 1914. Wing Commander Ireland was one of the commanding officers at Great Yarmouth for a time before his promotion to squadron commander took place in May 1915. Towards the end of the year he married Myrtle Lloyd.

He was killed in the same accident as Wing Commander Usborne in February the following year and was buried in Gillingham.

Herbert Carmichael IRWIN was a flight sub-lieutenant at Kingsnorth in February 1916.

Reginald Eric Victor JELLIFFE was a flight sub-lieutenant at Kingsnorth in February 1916.

Allan LANMAN was a warrant officer posted to Kingsnorth in August 1915.

Arthur Raymond LAYARD was a lieutenant RNVR at Kingsnorth in February 1916.

H.T.P. LEFROY was commissioned in the Royal Engineers in 1899 and began to study wireless communication at Gibraltar in 1905. The wireless sets used by the army were quite large and heavy and Lefroy worked on the specific problems presented by the need to provide wireless communication in aircraft.

In October 1909, Captain Lefroy was placed in charge of all experimental work in wireless telegraphy for the army, a post he retained until the outbreak of the First World War. In January 1911 he went up in the newly commissioned army airship *Beta*, which he had equipped with wireless apparatus, from Farnborough. Messages could be sent up to a range of 30 miles but engine noise made it impossible to hear incoming messages while the airship was under power. Captain Lefroy continued to work on the problem of receiving messages with the aircraft engine running and by 1913 had designed a new receiving set which reduced disturbances and strengthened the incoming signal. When it was tested during army manoeuvres between airships *Delta* and *Eta*, he was able to report that the airships could exchange messages with each other when 100 miles apart in the air. Lefroy himself received clear signals from about 130 miles away.

Major Lefroy was still in the armed forces in 1924 when he was one of a number of officials who witnessed a demonstration of Harry Grindell Matthews's 'Death Ray'. He was head of wireless research at the Air Ministry when he was involved as part of an investigating committee engaged in examining the electronic reactions of Abrams and the emanometer technique which reported to the Royal Society for medicine in 1925.

Cecil LEICESTER was a petty officer at Kingsnorth before moving to a nearby aerodrome, where he was promoted to probationary observer officer.

Ivor Cecil LITTLE was born in October 1895. He was appointed a midshipman in the Royal Navy during May 1915. Transferring to the RNAS, he was appointed a flight sub-lieutenant and posted to Kingsnorth in August 1915. He gained favourable reports of his work in airships at Kingsnorth and in February 1916 he was posted to Longside, Aberdeen. By the time he was awarded his certificate as an airship pilot in early October of 1916, he had amassed 360 hours' flying time.

Recommended for being 'a very good Rigid Airship Officer' at Howden in June of the following year, he was advanced to flight lieutenant and moved to the airship station at Barrow-in-Furness, where he commenced work on a pioneering programme to attach a Sopwith Camel as a defensive aircraft to an airship, probably inspired by the earlier work he had seen being done at Kingsnorth. It was no doubt as a result of his subsequent design, the Little-Crook anchoring gear, conceived with a fellow officer, that he was invited to join the staff at the Airship Experimental Station at Pulham, Norfolk, in October 1917. Here, as CO of the *R23*, he carried out many trials, latterly as a temporary major in the newly established Royal Air Force, and by late 1918 Camel aircraft were indeed being 'slipped' from the *R23*. Such was the success of the experiments that Little applied to patent his design in July 1919, a patent which was duly approved and also covered the use of aircraft as auxiliary power plants for airships. He was awarded the AFC. For further information, see Philip Jarrett's article 'At the Drop of a Camel' in *The Cross & Cockade* (Vol.VIII, No. 3, 1977, GB edition), a definitive account of these early trials.

After the war, Little remained employed on airship duties, carrying out numerous test flights in the *R32* and the *R80*, Barnes Wallis being a passenger of his on at least one occasion. In July 1919, in the *R34*, he was among those to complete the first ever airship transatlantic crossing. As no one in the United States had much experience of handling big airships, Little carried out a parachute descent on the *R34's* arrival at Lakehurst, New Jersey, in order to give instructions to the US Navy handling party.

Accordingly, he was an ideal candidate for the next big transatlantic project, the *R38*. Constructed at the Royal Airship Works at Cardington, the *R38* made her maiden flight in June 1921, when defects were found in her framework. As a result, further test flights were undertaken in the lead-up to her proposed journey to New Jersey, where she was to be handed over to the Americans and renamed *ZR2*. And it was in the course of one of these tests that she blew up over the River Humber at 5.40 p.m. on 21 August 1921. A trawler 16 miles away staggered under the shockwaves of the explosion and trains on railway lines in Lincolnshire shook on their tracks, while ceilings in houses in Hull and Grimsby collapsed. Only four of her forty-eight passengers survived. The death toll included sixteen members of the US Navy's Rigid Airship Detachment and many highly experienced British airship personnel, not least Air Commodore E.M. Maitland CMG, DSO, AFC, and Flight Lieutenants Little, Montagu, Pritchard and Thomas, in addition to Constructor Commander Campbell of the Royal Airship Works. Little's body was recovered on 29 August and interred in a common grave with Maitland, Campbell and a leading aircraftman in Hull Western Cemetery on 3 September.

John L. LONGSTAFF entered the Air Service on 6 January 1916 and was posted straight to Kingsnorth, where the February Navy List records him. On 25 May 1916 he was appointed to the post of 'AVG executive officer'. Lieutenant Commander Longstaff was brought before a court martial on 10 October 1916, charged with being 'Drunk on Shore', and, 'Acting to the prejudice of good order and naval discipline in creating a disturbance'. Had he been drunk and disorderly on the base, it seems no one would have been unduly bothered, but being drunk off-base was detrimental to the reputation of the navy, and this was compounded by the fact that he was an officer. He pleaded guilty and was sentenced to forfeit one year's seniority and was dismissed from HMS *President II*. He left Kingsnorth, the RNAS and probably the navy as well, as his dismissal was written in big red letters at the end of his short service record. This was clearly the kind of incident Commander Usborne hoped to avoid when he requested a wet canteen on the base, to keep the men away from the 'low alehouses' of the district.

Maurice Aldous LOVELL was a flight sub-lieutenant at Kingsnorth in February 1916.

Ian MACDONALD was a flight sub-lieutenant at Kingsnorth in February 1916.

Angus James Hugh McCOLL was a flight sub-lieutenant at Kingsnorth in February 1916.

Alan Grandaze McEWAN joined the navy on 1 September 1914 and transferred to the RNAS on 13 May 1915, training at Kingsnorth until 2 October. He served at several airship stations but seems to have made the most impression at Polegate. He had two more stints at Kingsnorth, from 21 June 1916 and 6 October 1916 to 6 September 1917.

F.M. McWADE, the resident inspector at the Aeronautical Inspection Department of the Royal Airship Works, was born in Glasgow in 1872. He was trained at the School of Military Engineering and joined the School of Ballooning, Royal Engineers, in 1895. He took part in the building of the airship *Nulli Secundus* in 1903 and also assisted in later years in the construction of airships *Beta*, *Gamma*, *Delta* and *Eta*. In 1915 he was engaged at Kingsnorth Airship Station on the building of non-rigids.

From 1920 to 1924 McWade was an 'AID officer' at the experimental seaplane stations at the Isle of Grain and Felixstowe, after which he became resident inspector at the Royal Airship Works at Cardington and was responsible for the close inspection of the airship *R101* during her construction. He refused to pass it as fit for flight in September 1930 and when officials pushed through his objections he was proved right as the airship crashed, killing nearly everyone on board. McWade was supposed to be on this flight but apparently decided against boarding, he testified at the hearing. Airships *R102*, *R103* and *R104* were planned but with many of the design team and experienced crew dead they were never built. In 1931, the government decided to abandon its rigid airship programme and McWade disappeared from public view.

Percy Eric MAITLAND, born on 26 October 1895 in Alverstoke, Hampshire, joined the navy in 1908, and by 1911 he was a naval cadet at Dartmouth. He was a midshipman on HMS *Dreadnought* in 1914, transferred to the RNAS on 17 May 1915, and served at Barrow and Capel before transferring to Kingsnorth, where he was trained on Coastals between 17 June and 26 August 1916. After that he served at Longside and East Fortune.

After the First World War he continued working in the airship branch of the RAF until they abandoned the airship programme. His specialisation was navigation and between the wars he served in Egypt and Iraq, flying the airmail route from Cairo to Baghdad, before he became navigator on a record-breaking flight to Australia. He served as commanding officer in a number of posts during the Second World War and continued in the service for several years after the end of the war before requesting retirement. Air Vice-Marshal P.E. Maitland died in Wallingford on 22 August 1985.

Joseph Stephen MIDDLETON was born in West Ham, on the outskirts of London, towards the end of March 1890. He trained as an engineer's turner. He was involved with airship experiments at Farnborough and was transferred to Kingsnorth when the work moved there. He worked with Wing Commander Cave-Brown-Cave and in a 1972 interview with an oral-history collector at the Imperial War Museum explained the difficulties in getting the fuselage in the correct position under the envelope during the development of the SS airship. The work was painfully slow because each time they had to move one of the Eta patches, to find the optimum position for balance and stability, not only did they have to carefully remove it without damaging the envelope but had to wait twenty-four hours for the glue to dry once it had been reattached in the new position. This did not only involve the attachment of the car to the envelope but also to all the control cables, as correct tension was vital to their operation. It took nearly a month to get it right, after which it was a relatively easy job for the other ships to be assembled using *SS1* as a pattern.

Having worked on the *SS1*, Middleton then worked on the Coastal-class ships. Their cars were much boxier than those of the SS airships. The initial design was good except that the wiring was too light and they had to rewire the whole chassis with heavier-gauge wire. Between April and September 1916, he flew Coastal airships at Longside before joining Commander Masterman's test crew flying various rigid airships. He was posted to East Fortune from January to May 1917, flying anti-submarine patrols with *R24*.

He died at Crawley in Sussex during the autumn of 1984, aged 94.

Louis D. MORRISON entered the RNAS on 20 April 1916 and was trained at Wormwood Scrubs. On 10 July he was sent to Kingsnorth for further instruction and then on 7 November he moved on to Howden.

Athol Wordsworth MYLNE was born on 11 December 1894. He joined the Royal Navy as a cadet and trained at Dartmouth, joining the RNAS on 17 March 1915. His first posting to Kingsnorth was on 18 September 1915. On 28 November 1916 he was noted there flying *NS2*. On 1 April 1917 he volunteered as an experimental test pilot. He was described as 'very committed' and on 23 July 1917 he was the pilot for *NS4*. He was moved to Pulham and East Fortune, and was awarded a permanent commission in the RAF on 22 January 1920.

During the inter-war period, his career in the RAF progressed steadily and by 1939 he was the commanding officer at RAF Leconfield. By the end of the

Second World War, Air Commodore Mylne was assistant/deputy Air Officer in charge of Administration (AOA) at HQ Bomber Command. He retired on 21 May 1945 and died on 11 April 1979.

Reverend Charles John Eyre PESHALL was born in Oldberrow Rectory, Henley-in-Arden, Warwickshire on 13 November 1881 and educated at Haileybury College, Great Amwell, Hertfordshire. Reverend Peshall MA became a naval chaplain in May 1908 and travelled to Australia, amongst other places, over the next four years.

He had served with Captain Davidson and seen active service on HMS *Cornwallis* before transferring to the RNAS, serving with No. 3 wing. He arrived at Kingsnorth Airship Station on Saturday 26 May 1917 to become the first resident station chaplain. A keen believer in the spiritual benefits of hymn-singing, one of his first actions was to ask for volunteers to form a choir, and he also assured the men that, although he was lodged with the officers, they should not hesitate to approach him should they need advice or assistance. As well as looking after the spiritual welfare of the men, Rev. Peshall was also a keen sportsman.

After the war he married Beatrice Docker, and they had two children, John and Julia. He was based in Portsmouth between 1929 and 1931, and by 1935 he had become an archdeacon and was awarded the King George V Silver Jubilee Medal to go with his CBE and DSO.

His wife died in London in April 1944. In 1949 he was listed as a retired chaplain of the fleet. Rev. Peshall died in Westminster in 1957 in his mid-seventies.

Edmund Walker Rennie PINKNEY, born on 28 January 1876, was a member of a prominent Sunderland family of shipbuilders. The *London Gazette* for 23 February 1906 lists him as a second lieutenant in the 3rd Volunteer Battalion of the Northumberland Fusiliers.

He was awarded a DSO on 1 January 1917 before he became the principal technical advisor to the officer in charge at Kingsnorth on 5 November 1917. The *London Gazette* mentions him again on 9 September 1918: 'Lt.-Col. E.W.R. Pinkney, D.S.O., from T.F. Res., to be Lt.-Col., with precedence as from 15 August 1914.' He was awarded the Territorial Decoration on 30 May 1919.

After the war, he returned to shipbuilding and was a director of Swan Hunter & Wigham Richardson. He was appointed Deputy Lieutenant of Northumberland on 8 May 1924 and retired from the Territorial Army with the rank of colonel on 18 March 1933. He lived at Jesmond, Newcastle-upon-Tyne, until his death on 21 October 1940.

John E.M. PRITCHARD was born at Leighton Buzzard, Bedfordshire, in 1889. He was educated privately and at Cambridge, where he took an MA. Following a postgraduate course at the Royal School of Mines, he was elected a fellow of the Royal Geological Society, and then took up his career as a mining engineer. He married Hilda Elizabeth Caldwell Smith in Putney on 2 October 1913.

When war broke out, Pritchard joined the RNAS as flight sub-lieutenant. He was posted to Roehampton Kite Balloon Station, and passed out in ballooning and aerostatics. In 1915 he was posted to Kingsnorth, and later to Polegate, in command of *SS9*. Early in 1916 he was posted to RNAS Mudros in the eastern Mediterranean, in command of *SS3*, where he made a Mediterranean airship record of eight hours' flying. Late in 1916 he was posted to Polegate again, this time as senior flying and experimental officer.

In January of 1917 he was sent to East Fortune airship station as commanding officer of *C24*. Two months later he was transferred to Howden as commanding officer of the Parseval airship *P6*, and in August of the same year he was posted to Cranwell. September 1917 saw him posted to the Admiralty Airship Department for rigid acceptance pilot and technical flying duties. During the latter part of 1917 and in 1918, he examined the various airships brought down and wrote reports on them, as well as translating notebooks, logbooks and so on found on board, or on the crews. As technical airship officer, he went to Germany after the Armistice, and in 1919 he was Admiralty Airship Representative to the Peace Conference in Paris.

He made the flight to America and back in *R34*, jumping out with a parachute to give instructions to the landing party on the US side. From October 1919, he was acceptance pilot, and did technical flying duties under the Airship Experimental and Research Division of the Air Ministry.

Major Pritchard was keenly interested in the internal combustion engine, and he had great faith in the slow-running 'heavy oil' diesel engine for airship work. He was a strong advocate of the Ricardo engine, and used all his influence to obtain extensive research work on engines of this type. Like a good many other airship experts, he was of the opinion that the greatest danger to airships arose from the petrol fumes and not from the hydrogen, hence his desire to see the heavy-oil engine developed.

Major Jack Pritchard OBE, AFC died in 1921 in the *R38* accident at Hull. This accident is described in the entry for Ivor Cecil Little (pp. 127–8).

Stanley Edward RITCHIE was born on 27 February 1896. He entered the RNAS on 24 October 1914 and trained at Farnborough before being posted to Barrow on 3 March 1915. The following month he was sent to Kingsnorth and was promoted to acting flight lieutenant on 7 May 1915 before returning to Barrow on 23 May. His promotion to flight lieutenant was confirmed a month later. On 16 October 1915 he came back to Kingsnorth for six months and was then posted to Longside, 'proficient to proceed on Active Service'. His CO at Longside remarked on his good ability to command and great initiative powers, adding that he would make a very good officer. On 2 September 1916 he graduated as an airship pilot at Wormwood Scrubs, and three days later his CO at Longside was again praising his initiative and described him as a first-rate airship pilot.

A month later he returned to Barrow in the rigid-airship trial party, where he was recommended for promotion for his zeal, marked efficiency, initiative and tact. At the end of 1916 his promotion to flight commander was noted.

On 4 April 1917 he was posted to Howden, where he was described as a very good rigid airship officer. He applied to transfer to heavier-than-air craft on 27 September, and although the Admiralty made no objection, they did note that this was not to be taken as a precedent and questioned whether he should retain his rank upon transferring. Three weeks later he was posted to Manston Flying School and on 30 December went to Cranwell for more instruction. Near the end of January 1918, he fractured his fibula and was off for a couple of months. Another month at Cranwell was followed by three weeks at Redcar instructors' school, before he was posted to Eastbourne on 13 May 1918.

Leslie ROBINS, the son of Engineer Rear Admiral Samuel Robins, was born on 17 October 1879. He joined the Royal Navy on 1 July 1894, going straight into the RN Engineering College at Devonport. A career sailor, he was serving on a light cruiser, HMS *Amethyst*, at the beginning of the First World War. He was transferred to on-shore duties, first at Chatham's engineering department, and later at Rosyth.

In December 1916 Robins was posted to Kingsnorth, and was involved in trials of the first Submarine Scout Pusher (SSP) airship in January 1917 and the North Sea airship the following month. By March, Leslie had gained 'considerable experience' of airships and on 20 March his commanding officer confirmed him in the post of chief engineer.

His service record of 5 October 1917 shows him still at Kingsnorth, but under the Deputy Controller of Armament Production (DCAP) on 1 April 1918 he is recorded as lieutenant colonel in the Royal Air Force List. In August 1918, the Air Ministry said they did not wish him to be attached to the RAF and his name would not appear in the RAF List in future.

In November 1918, improved Coastal airships were under construction, but production was concentrated on the Sea Scout Twin, with forty-seven in the pipeline. This programme was rapidly cut back once peace was declared.

On 11 June 1919, Robins's OBE award was announced in the *London Gazette* for 'valuable services throughout the war, particularly in connection with the design and construction of machinery for airships'. The full recommendation states:

> In the Department of Airship Construction was Head of Section dealing with design and construction of machinery for rigid and non-rigid airships, and machinery equipment for airship stations, and has since been responsible for the work of that section, including the introduction of a special type of airship engine. He has done consistently good work in connection with the design and supply of engines for both rigid and non-rigid airships. The able manner in which he has organised his department has resulted in a great degree in the efficiency of airships and the marked success with which they have been maintained in commission.

Returning to waterborne ships after the war, Robins continued to work in engineering and was promoted to rear admiral just before his retirement on 1 May 1930. On 5 March 1940 he took up the post of Admiralty Officer in the North-West, based at Piccadilly House, Piccadilly, Manchester, until 30 November 1945. Leslie died on 14 February 1949 at Victoria Cottage Hospital, Emsworth.

Richard Stirling ROBINSON was born in April 1886 and entered the Royal Navy, receiving advancement to lieutenant in December 1908. He was wounded in August 1914.

He joined the RNAS on 28 February 1916 and trained at Wormwood Scrubs before being posted to Kingsnorth on 14 April 1916 to pilot *SS14*. Between 11 and 13 November 1916 he was up to mischief, as his service record shows he 'Incurred T.L's severe Displeasure in connection with the misuse of Rover Touring Car 1146 at Kingsnorth'. Affectionately known as Commander Robbie, he was the officer commanding *NS1* during its troubled trial flight on 2 February 1917. TL seems to have forgiven him the misdemeanour with the Rover as on 13 July 1917 it is written, 'Expression of T.L's appreciation in connection with the endurance flight carried out in airship *NS1* on 26 June at Pulham'. In May 1918 he was a temporary lieutenant colonel in the RAF and flying *SSZ57*.

He was awarded the OBE in June 1919. He died in December 1942.

F. Woodis ROGERS (Captain, RAF) was the station hydrogen officer, editing *Flighty*, in July 1918, and there is a sketch of him wearing a monocle in one edition, along with the information that as well as editing the newsletter he was a member of the boxing committee and a keen gardener.

F. Michael ROPE was born in 1888 at Shrewsbury and was educated at Shrewsbury School and Birmingham University, where he took an engineering degree. He left the University in 1910 and until 1912 was an engineer to the British Electric Plant Co., Alloa. He then joined Rio Tinto, the London-headquartered mining and mechanical-engineering firm. From 1913 to 1914 he was employed in locomotive engineering by the London, Brighton & South Coast Railway and from then to 1915 served in the same capacity with the Nigerian Railway Corporation in west Africa.

He joined the RNAS in 1915, serving at Capel and Kingsnorth stations, where he subsequently became staff officer in the Director of Research's department. Somewhere around this time he transferred to the RAF, was promoted to the rank of squadron leader and from 1921 to 1924 he was technical staff officer, RAF, in Iraq. Rope was then appointed to the Royal Airship Works, Cardington, and was seconded from the Royal Air Force in 1930. By then he was assistant to Lieutenant Colonel Richmond, Assistant Director (Technical). As such he was on the doomed flight of *R101* and died in the crash. A photo of Squadron Leader Rope can be seen on the Shortstown Heritage website.

George Herbert SCOTT was born on 25 May 1888 in Catford, Kent, educated at Richmond School, Yorkshire, and the Royal Naval Engineering College, Keyham. From 1908 he was engaged in general engineering until the outbreak of war when he joined the Royal Naval Air Service as a flight sub-lieutenant. After service at Farnborough in HMA *Eta* and at Kingsnorth, he proceeded in 1915 to the airship station at Barrow and became captain of the Parseval *P4*. On 9 August 1916 he was unfit for duty for nearly two months, suffering with varicose veins. The following year he was appointed to the command of the airship station at Anglesey and in 1917

(RAF Museum, Hendon)

became captain of *R9*, and was also appointed experimental officer, airships, at Pulham airship base. On the formation of the Royal Air Force he was given the rank of major.

Towards the end of 1918 he was chosen to command *R34* and was awarded the AFC for his work on airships. In 1919 he commanded *R34* on its flight from East Fortune, Scotland, to the United States and back to Pulham. For this he was awarded the CBE. This was the first east-to-west crossing of the Atlantic, just a month after Alcock and Brown crossed from Newfoundland to Ireland in a modified Vickers Vimy bomber, and the first crossing to carry passengers.

He was demobilised from the Royal Air Force later in 1919. In 1920 he was appointed to the technical staff of the Royal Airship Works, Cardington. He was the inventor of the Air Ministry's system of airship mooring to a tower, which is also employed in the United States. In 1924 he was appointed officer in charge of flying and training in the Airship Directorate and in January of that year became assistant director (flying). He visited Canada in 1927 to advise the Canadian government on the selection of an airship base, which resulted in Saint Hubert, Montreal, being chosen and equipped. He carried out extended trials of the two new British airships, *R101* and *R100*, the largest airships in the world at the time, which contained many novel features compared with previous airship types. On Sunday 5 October 1930, Major Scott was in command of the *R101* when it crashed in flames at Beauvais, France. Only five of the fifty-four people on board survived. This crash and the loss of Major Scott marked the end of the airship programme.

Henry Sydney SCROGGS was born in 1896, trained as a cadet at the Osborne Cadet School and followed his father into the navy in 1913, serving aboard HMS *Monarch*. Midshipman Scroggs was selected for airship training and joined the RNAS on 17 March 1915. He was sent to Kingsnorth and trained there until 3 April. He then served at Anglesey, Howden, Capel and Pulham, rising to the rank of flight lieutenant. He revisited Kingsnorth between 12 August and 29 September for Coastal work.

Captain Scroggs was transferred to the RAF and continued in their service between the wars, playing in the RAF rugby team in 1919–20 and serving in Egypt at one point. He was promoted to squadron leader in 1929 and from 1934 to 1936 was stationed at the Far East Command HQ as navigation staff officer, after which came another promotion to wing commander. After the outbreak of the Second World War he was promoted to group captain and was in command of the RAF station on Thorney Island, Sussex, when, on 29 September 1941, he was killed on active service.

Francis Blewet SHAW was a married man from Bodmin when he joined the RNAS in December 1914. His first posting was to White City as a temporary armoured cars lieutenant. In February 1916 he went on courses to Sunbeam Works and Talbot Works before being posted to the Rolls-Royce works at Kingsnorth the following month. On 2 October 1916, Shaw was demobilised 'in order that he may be loaned to tank supply Dept. of the Ministry of Munitions'.

Richard Vynne SOUTHWELL was probably involved in experimental engineering. He retired from the RAF with the rank of major and became one of the vice-presidents of the Kingsnorth Gasbags. The address he gave in the 1935 edition of *Flighty* was Engineering Laboratory, Parks Road, Oxford.

Francis Warrington STRONG was born in Whitby, North Yorkshire, in the spring of 1892. He entered service in the RNAS on 18 August 1914 and was posted to White City as a wireless telegraphist. On 7 May 1915 he was promoted to the rank of flight lieutenant and at the beginning of the following month was posted to Cranwell. On 12 February 1917 he went to the Air Department 'T' section and on 9 August moved on to Kingsnorth for wireless telegraphy duties. He appears to have remained at Kingsnorth for some time thereafter.

He died on 28 June 1967.

Ronald Scott SUGDEN was born on 25 May 1896, and entered the RNAS on 13 May 1915. By 20 July 1916 he was an experienced pilot and was sent from Polegate to Kingsnorth to be captain of the *C15*. He served at Polegate and East Fortune before returning to Kingsnorth on 24 September 1917 to assist in detail work on the new Coastal design. On 12 December he went to Crystal Palace for the 'E' course and was then transferred to Pulham and Cranwell. He continued in the RAF after the war.

In 1927 his engagement to Helen Mary Brain, who lived near Cardiff, was announced. They subsequently married and had a daughter, Mary Susan. Sugden was a keen cricketer, playing for the RAF team in 1929. He was promoted to the rank of wing commander in 1936 and had been promoted to group captain by the time he was awarded a CBE in June 1945. He died in Dinas Powys on 26 March 1971.

Richard SWALLOW was a coxswain at Kingsnorth in its early days, gaining a huge amount of experience on airship construction and rigging. Dick was part of the Kingsnorth erection party on North Sea airships before being gazetted as a probationary flight officer in the summer of 1917.

Charles Broughton Clay SWAYNE was born in Wiltshire during the last quarter of 1895. A midshipman in 1913, he transferred into the RNAS on 17 March 1915 and served at Kingsnorth between 3 January and 26 September 1916. His first request to revert to sea service was denied on 23 March 1916 but a second request was approved and he returned to sea on 26 February 1917.

In 1924 he was serving on HMS *Greenwich*, an 8,600-ton destroyer repair ship.

He was a commander when he died at Chatham while on active service, on 7 November 1942.

Godfrey Maine THOMAS joined the navy and was passed out as a midshipman on 15 January 1913. Next to his name are the initials KM. This medal was awarded to him for having 'exhibited the most gentleman like bearing and good influence among the cadets' during his training. He went into the RNAS and was posted to Kingsnorth between 17 March 1915 and 15 March 1916, before heading for the Dardanelles. He returned for another stint at Kingsnorth between 8 September 1916 and 5 January 1917. By August 1917 he was an acting lieutenant based at Howden.

Edward Fisher TURNER became a midshipman in the navy on 15 September 1913, entered the RNAS on 17 March 1915 and was at Kingsnorth until 20 May. After this two-month training period, he was posted elsewhere, serving longest at Cranwell. He returned to Kingsnorth on 9 February 1918 for further training to become captain of the *C*18*. He was transferred away again on 3 April 1918 and was elected as a member of the Royal Aero Club on 18 February 1919.

Flight magazine for 8 January 1936 reports the promotion of Edward Fisher Turner AFC from squadron leader to wing commander.

Edward Keith Henry TURNOUR was born in Wales around 1896. In 1913 he was a midshipman on the battleship HMS *Collingwood*. Turnour joined the RNAS on 17 March 1915, training at Kingsnorth until 3 April before transferring to Luce Bay and Howden.

He returned to Wales before he died in 1968.

Wilfred UNDERHILL was a navy cadet in 1911. By 15 May 1913 he was a midshipman, transferring to the RNAS on 13 May 1915. He went to Anglesey before being posted to Kingsnorth, where he trained between 28 July and 4 September 1916, and then moved on to Longside. On 1 May 1918 his commanding officer recommended Flight Lieutenant Underhill for a DSC for his work on long-range airships. He was promoted from flight lieutenant to flight commander at the beginning of January 1918.

Archibald Herbert WANN was born on 26 November 1895, and joined the Royal Navy as a cadet in 1908. He was promoted to midshipman on 15 May 1913 and in 1915 went to Wormwood Scrubs to train as an airship pilot. Before the end of the year he had been posted to Kingsnorth and then on to Polegate. He later moved on to East Fortune. On 1 August 1919 Wann was awarded a permanent commission with the rank of flight lieutenant. The following year he joined the staff at Pulham, the experimental airship station. On 20 January he was removed from the Navy Lists and awarded a permanent commission in the RAF, moving to the staff of RAF airship base Howden on 21 March the same year. He commanded the *R36* and the *R38* and was the only officer to survive the *R38* explosion over the Humber in August 1921 (see p. 128).

On 24 February 1922 he became a 'supernumerary' at HQ Coastal Area and was placed on half-pay between 13 April and 13 June the same year before being posted as a supernumerary at an RAF depot on 16 June. On 7 September he moved again, as a supernumerary at the RAF School of Naval Co-operation and Aerial Navigation.

5 February 1923 saw Wann moved again, this time as a member of staff at RAF Calshot. On 11 November the following year he was promoted to officer commanding the School of Balloon Training. On 10 May 1926, he attended RAF Staff College and on 6 January 1928 was moved to the staff of the Deputy Directorate of Manning. He acted as registrar during the Court of Inquiry into the loss of the *R101* in 1930. His narrow escape nine years earlier gave him a special insight into such crashes.

On 4 January 1932 he attended a flying boat pilot's course at RAF Calshot. He was placed on half-pay between 7 and 19 August later that year but on 20 August became the commanding officer of No. 202 Squadron.

By 30 May 1934 he was once more placed as a supernumerary at the RAF depot before joining the staff of the Directorate of Staff Duties. He stayed there for about four years until, around 1938, he was promoted to Deputy Director of Operations (Naval Co-operation). He moved again the following year to become a wing commander in the Advanced Air Strike Force.

On 20 December 1940 he was noted as an RAF commanding officer in Northern Ireland, and while there he conducted experimental exercises with Colonel J.D. Woodhall in Army/Air Co-operation. These exercises led to the 'Wann-Woodhall' report, which formed the basis for the operations of Army Co-operation Command when it emerged in late 1940.

On 22 April 1941, Wann became a group captain at Fighter Command. Two years later, on 26 March 1943, he became Air Officer Commanding No. 212 Group and in September the following year he was Director of Personnel (Morale and Rehabilitation).

Archibald Wann died in France on 11 October 1948.

Walter Kerneys Francis Goodhall WARNEFORD was born on 19 July 1895. He entered the RNAS on 24 October 1914, starting in the kite balloon section. He was promoted to acting flight lieutenant on 7 May 1915 and served at Anglesey, Capel and Longside before graduating as an airship pilot at Wormwood Scrubs on 16 September 1916. He only served at Kingsnorth for a month during November 1916 on *C24* before being transferred to East Fortune to captain *C25*.

Warneford was promoted to the rank of flight commander on 30 June 1917 and continued to receive good reports from his CO at East Fortune. Shortly before the formation of the Royal Air Force he was captain of the *NS4*. At the age of 24 he was captain of the *NS11* when, at the beginning of February 1919, it set a world endurance record during a 4,000-mile mine-hunting patrol, and during its last flight five months later, another mine-hunting patrol which would take it down as far as Kingsnorth and possibly regain the endurance record, which had just been beaten by *R34*. As *NS11* was en route, her radio malfunctioned. This may have contributed to her attracting the lightning strike that resulted in a huge explosion off the coast near Pulham with the loss of all on board.

Francis WARRINGTON-STRONG served as a captain at Kingsnorth towards the end of the war. He was also the editor of *Flighty*, the station newsletter, in July 1918. After the war he became one of the vice-presidents of the Kingsnorth Gasbags.

Clive Maitland WATERLOW was born on 9 September 1885. Waterlow was experienced with lighter-than-air flight before joining the RNAS on 1 January 1914, as he had been at the Balloon School from 1906 to 1910. On 24 January 1911 he passed his RAC Certificate on Airship *No. 3* and was a member of the Air Battalion in 1912 and the RFC by 1913. This wealth of experience meant that his rank in the newly formed RNAS was that of squadron commander. He moved from Farnborough to Kingsnorth with the 'balloons' and was there until the end of January 1916, when he was moved to become the commanding officer at Wormwood Scrubs.

At the end of 1916 he was due to join the exam board for promotion of ratings, but this was cancelled and instead he was posted to Cranwell on 19 February 1917. This is where he was when he married Winifred Joan Clare on 9 June that year. His death at Cranwell, while trying to moor an airship, on 20 July 1917 was one of the many tragic airship accidents that occurred during the war.

John Sylvester WHEELWRIGHT was born on 25 July 1885 at Burnt Oak Farm, Edgware, Middlesex. He was the son of John Joseph Hanley Wheelwright, an Englishman who had until recently been a sheep-station owner and operator at Darling Downs in Queensland, Australia. Driven home by an Australian drought in the late 1870s, 'Jack' was the youngest of ten. His grandfather and two of his older brothers were professional artists so it was no surprise that Jack displayed a youthful flair for art and design.

At the outbreak of war in 1914, he volunteered for service in the Royal Navy, becoming a flight sub-lieutenant on 15 April 1915 (*London Gazette*) and a distinguished airship pilot in the RNAS, flying patrols in areas as diverse as the Dardanelles and the North Sea, where he set several new flying records. Flight Lieutenant Wheelwright was transferred to Kingsnorth for the first time in April 1916 and whilst at the station he contributed ideas for the design of the Coastal-class airships. On 26 May 1916 he was given *C17* for her first test flight and he transferred with her when she was sent to Pulham three months later. On 6 March 1917 Jack returned to Kingsnorth, where he was soon putting his technical skills to good use, designing instruments to improve the accuracy of navigation. On 1 October 1917, now a flight commander, he was awarded the Distinguished Service Cross for services on patrol duties and submarine-searching in home waters (*London Gazette*) and, in 1918, narrowly escaped a fatal crash. By 3 June 1918 he was a lieutenant (temporary captain) and was mentioned in dispatches (*London Gazette*). By 1919 he was senior flying officer at the non-rigid airship construction station at Kingsnorth, where he developed and improved the iconic French Caquot 'pear-drop' barrage balloon, finally designing and building the first internal-expansion balloon to be constructed in Britain.

When the Great War ended, Jack Wheelwright returned to his old job, spending the next two decades creating designs for domestic wallpapers and fabric as well as filing dozens of engineering patents for new printing machinery.

It was with these credentials that he volunteered again to join the RAF in 1939. Having been an auxiliary in the interwar years, he was promoted from the rank of major to squadron leader on 16 May 1938 (*London Gazette*) and on 6 June 1939 to wing commander and given command of 901 Squadron.

He continued his work to design and produce experimental balloons, constructing prototypes from surplus or salvaged parts from London balloon stations. He showed that his high-zone balloon could be successfully flown at altitudes of 10,000ft and more, yet the established scientific community were hard to convince and, for the most part, failed to support his research. Released from military service on the grounds of his age in 1942, Jack went freelance and, with the personal endorsement of the prime minister, produced designs for a further half-dozen military machines – invariably aimed at the preservation, rather than the destruction, of life. He died later that year, an inventor to the end (see *A Man of Invention* by S.J. Plummer).

Thomas Blenheim WILLIAMS was born on 15 January 1892. After an initial period of primary training at Wormwood Scrubs and Hurlingham, Williams moved on to further training at Kingsnorth at the beginning of June 1916. His first impressions were that it was a much more formal and efficient establishment. This was primarily because all the staff there were residential and the station was run as a ship, with naval parlance used: for example, if you wished to go  off-base, you would ask permission to go ashore. Kingsnorth was twice the size of Wormwood Scrubs; by this date the station was just about finished. There were two large sheds and three airships operated out of the station: two Submarine Scouts and the first of the Coastals.

The training at Kingsnorth took about a month. Williams was an enthusiastic student and was very high up in the list of passes, as was a fellow student named Taylor, both qualifying as airship pilots around 5 July. He was delighted to be given command of *SS31*, a Maurice Farman Pusher, while Taylor was given command of *SS14*, a BE2c tractor with the engine at the front. Williams was delighted with his ship and was teased by the other pilots, who suggested he stayed up all night in the shed dusting it, but he just thought they were jealous.

SS31 was popularly known as a 'flying bedstead' due to its tendency to drift sideways in flight. A lot of experimental work was carried out on these airships to improve performance. There were numerous experiments to enable the ships to be moored out in the open, and also some aimed at decreasing the weight of the craft, leading to a number of hair-raising incidents that tested the pilots' skills to the limit. Williams also joined the team of officers training new pilots. Although qualified to pilot Coastal-class ships, Williams preferred the SS class, describing the bigger ships as sluggish.

In November 1916, Williams was transferred to Anglesey and a year later he was one of the crew sent to Ciampino in Italy to collect the newly purchased semi-rigid airship *SR1*.

On 19 August 1972, Williams was interviewed during an oral-history project at the Imperial War Museum. This led, in 1974, to a publication of his experiences as an airship pilot, which provided a lot of useful information regarding Kingsnorth (see Sources: Primary on p. 161).

Frank Geoffrey Eric WISEMAN was born on 17 February 1895. He was working as a bank clerk in 1911. In 1915 he joined the navy as a midshipman and on 18 March he arrived at Eastchurch with the rank of flight sub-lieutenant. Posted to Kingsnorth on 25 May, he was promptly suspended from flying on account of cramp. Wiseman was continually sick from the day he arrived and on 7 July was admitted to Chatham Hospital diagnosed with neuritis (inflammation of the nerves). On 10 December the medical officer reported that he was subject to fits, and 'might at any time have a seizure whilst flying. On making enquiries it transpires that the probable cause of this officer's illness was due to excessive consumption of intoxicants.' An order was given to the mess, limiting his consumption, and the fits seem to have abated.

Despite this, his CO, Squadron Commander Woodcock, wrote: 'I am of the opinion that he is not suitable for employment as a pilot for aircraft and that he does not exhibit the necessary qualities required of an officer. I consider that no good purpose can be served by his retention in the Air Service.' His appointment was terminated on 20 December 1915. Wiseman applied for reinstatement in June 1917 but was turned down.

RATINGS

Records for the rank and file are scarcer than those for officers so the list here, arranged again in alphabetical order, is just a small fraction of the hundreds of people who served on the base.

'Topsy' ABBOTS worked in the Kingsnorth transport department. It is not clear if she was a Wren (that is, a member of the Women's Royal Naval Service) or part of the civilian staff. Around Christmas 1918 she became engaged to Corporal H.C. Bond, who also worked in the transport department.

Walter ASHWELL was born in Purfleet, Essex, on 22 February 1892. An engine and crane driver by occupation, he enlisted in the RNAS on 26 October 1915. He served at Kingsnorth between October 1915 and January 1917, rated as an air mechanic first class and 'driver' and was then transferred to Howden, serving as a crewman of the airship *C20* from August to September 1917. Flight seems to have disagreed with him as his trade classification changed to hydrogen worker from December 1918. Ashwell served at Purfleet from March 1919 until he was transferred to the RAF Reserve on 30 April 1920.

Walter Herbert Victor BADGER was born in Peckham on 22 November 1883. He became a gas engineer (fitter/mechanic) and was married with a young son when war broke out. He was 30 years old when he joined up or was recruited to the Royal Navy and it would appear that, unusually, his skills as a gas engineer were pounced on and he was quickly sent off to work on airships. In 1914 he was living in Five Bells Lane, Hoo, and working at Kingsnorth.

After the war he moved back to London, living in Lewisham for about five years before moving out to Beckenham around 1924 and on to Farnborough around 1934. He died on 18 January 1962 at Bexhill, East Sussex.

B.A. BAGNALL, was sales manager for *Flighty*, the station newsletter, in July 1918. No mention was made of his official station duties.

Fred BECKETT was born around 1882 in Manchester, and worked as a gas-plant hand. Known to his friends and colleagues as 'Freddie', he was 34 when he drowned at Kingsnorth on 8 May 1917. For some reason he became stranded in a drifting boat. Despite the fact that he was an expert swimmer who had played water polo for Lancashire before the war, his attempt to swim to shore failed. On 6 July a benefit concert was held to raise funds to aid his widow.

William BISHOP, known by his friends as 'Bill', served at Kingsnorth before being transferred to a station on the Mediterranean.

H.C. BOND was a corporal in the Kingsnorth transport department around Christmas 1918, when he became engaged to Topsy Abbots, who worked in the same department.

Percy BROOKS was a member of the Kingsnorth working party before he was attached to No. 6 Wing and promoted to flight sergeant.

Thomas BUNCE was a leading mechanic at Kingsnorth who later moved to one of the northern stations.

E.S. CLARK was an air mechanic, who became honorary secretary of the Kingsnorth Orchestra when it was first set up in the early summer of 1917.

Albert COLLIER was a CPO mechanic, working with airships, and later qualified as an airship-crew member. There is no record as to whether he actually flew or not but his family had a photo of him in leather flying gear, sitting in what looks like an old motorcycle sidecar, suspended on cables from the underside of an airship. He served at Kingsnorth from some time in 1917 (the writing is very unclear) until 31 March 1918, when he was transferred to the RAF and became a sergeant mechanic (trade group: fitter).

DOOLE was an air mechanic, badly injured in a gas explosion in May 1917.

H.W. ELLIOTT was one of the editors of *Flighty*, the station newsletter, in July 1918.

Frank FLEMING wrote poetry for *Flighty* under the pen name 'Vera'. He was particularly mentioned in an article as attending a station dance and at first it appeared that Vera Fleming was one of the new Wrens on the station, but he was actually a member of the garage staff. After he left Kingsnorth, Fleming was involved in an accident that crushed one of his fingers and while on sick leave he returned to see his old comrades.

Harold FODEN moved from Kingsnorth to Dunkirk by 1917.

Joseph A. FREEMAN was a member of the Kingsnorth transport staff. Around the end of 1917 Joe transferred to the Royal Flying Corps, was promoted to second lieutenant and by the beginning of 1918 was under instruction at a flying school near Uxbridge.

H. Blake GEAKE was the honorary treasurer for *Flighty* in July 1918. Whether his accounting expertise came from his work on the station or his civilian occupation is unknown.

Sidney J. GEORGE, an air mechanic second class, died at Kingsnorth on 15 March 1917, as a result of an illness.

G.F. GILBERT was the sports representative for *Flighty* writing under the pseudonym 'The Filbert'. Before he joined the RNAS, Gilbert had been involved in the Herne Hill Harriers in Surrey, an amateur athletics club noted for cross-country running.

Charles E. GOFF, air mechanic second class, died at Kingsnorth on 9 September 1916 as a result of an illness.

Charles John GOODWILLIE was the son of a carpenter from Hammersmith and before the war he worked as a tea blender. He was 22 when war was declared and became a leading driver-mechanic at Kingsnorth. Charlie went on to train as a pilot and was transferred to a base in the Mediterranean.

After the war he worked as a chauffeur. He married Grace Willis in 1923, and they had a daughter the following year. They lived in Ealing. He was widowed in 1960 and died nineteen years later.

Robert H. HALL, known as 'Nobby', was a Metropolitan Police sergeant in a busy and not so salubrious part of London before the war. It is possible he had been in the navy earlier as he joined the Royal Fleet Reserve in 1902, serving aboard HMS *Canopus* in the Mediterranean. The Royal Fleet reserve was the naval equivalent of the Territorial Army, ensuring a body of trained men who could be called upon in time of need.

On 2 August 1914, Nobby was called up and served on HMS *Otranto* in the South Pacific, which took part in the battle of Coronel. In May 1915 he joined the staff at Kingsnorth as ship's barber. He then assisted the corporal of the guard until November, when he took over the duties of chief cook. His early days in this position were certainly challenging as the facilities at that time were less than ideal. He was featured in *Flighty* in June 1917, his biographer describing him as genial and sociable, good company anywhere and a fine singer.

Charles W. HARRIS, a leading mechanic at Kingsnorth, was killed on 27 May 1917 when the gas holder he was working on blew up. He was 38 years old. The inquest into his death was held on 2 June.

Jack HAYLON was born in Manchester on 18 October 1891. Before the war he had been an actor, using the stage name Jack Edge, and starred in a comedy film called *How's Your Poor Wife?*, which was shown at the station cinema. It is the only film he is known to appear in, though one suspects he must have had some supporting roles before getting top billing. At Kingsnorth, 'Jackie' was a member of the transport staff but after a stay of several months was posted to Kenley, much to the disappointment of the concert party.

M.B. HUGHES, a member of the RNVR, was a co-editor of *Flighty* for two issues in May and June 1918 before being posted afloat.

William J. JEFFREE came to Kingsnorth in July 1915 and spent two and a half years on the rigging party before volunteering for foreign service. Towards the end of 1918 he was stationed with an RNAS airship detachment near Salonica.

Albert JENNER was born on 27 Jan 1887 in Hollingbourne, Kent. On the census of 1901 he is at Well Street, Loose, Kent, where he was working as a factory hand. By 1911 he was working as a bricklayer before joining the RNAS as an aircraftman second class. While at Kingsnorth, he became ill and died on 3 Apr 1917, aged 29. He was buried at Gillingham (Woodlands) Cemetery.

Frederick David JOHNCOCK was born on 23 December 1889. He was 25 when war was declared and he joined up and became a leading mechanic. He married towards the end of 1914 in Reigate.

During his time on the airships, Fred collected together an album of photographs and information about his service during the First World War. He died in the spring of 1977. His album is now with the Fleet Air Arm Museum in Yeovilton.

(Fleet Air Arm Museum 2012/083/0011)

P.W. KEEN was an air mechanic and was the first conductor of the Kingsnorth Orchestra, which was started in the early summer of 1917.

Walter KNIGHT drove the Foden steam lorry at Kingsnorth, before being transferred to France. While working as a despatch rider there, he was knocked down by a French staff car and was sent back to England to recuperate.

J.B. LINKLATER was one of the two art editors for *Flighty* in July 1918.

Jack MADDOCKS moved from Kingsnorth to Dunkirk by 1917.

J.E. MARTIN joined Kingsnorth as a 'boy' rating. He was a consistent player in the station soccer team before he moved to Pulham as an air mechanic first class.

W.J. MIDDLETON DFM Middleton belonged to the 2nd Epping Forest Troop of Boy Scouts before the war, and was an assistant scoutmaster. When he left Kingsnorth he became a sergeant observer in France. He was shot in the abdomen when his ship was attacked while taking observations over enemy lines. His pilot got him straight back to the aerodrome and he was sent to hospital for an emergency operation but although he regained consciousness he didn't survive. His death was reported in the station magazine.

Patrick O'MARA was at Kingsnorth before being transferred to the Mediterranean.

Frederick George POLHILL was a cobbler and the son of a bootmaker. He was about 25 when he married Florence Susan Ann Shapcott in the early summer of 1915 in Edmonton, North London. Corporal Polhill's cobbling skills were soon put to good use when he arrived at Kingsnorth, as he started a sideline fixing footwear in his own time while attached to the guard, but the advantages of having a ship's cobbler were soon recognised, and when the new canteen and offices were built a room was provided for him in which to ply his trade.

When the war was over and Corporal Polhill was no doubt looking forward to returning to his wife and business, he was killed by the particularly virulent bout of influenza which swept through the station. His mates in B Room described him as, 'one of the cheeriest fellows we knew'. His many friends, knowing his business in London had suffered through being deprived of his attention during the war, arranged a benefit concert in aid of his widow and the Black and Whites put on a splendid show, which raised £50. Corporal Polhill was buried in Gillingham. An officer and twelve ratings attended his funeral, and his widow asked them to express her deep gratitude to the officers and men on the station for their generous support.

Charlie REGAN worked in the gas plant and was one of the Black and White concert party who put on some outdoor entertainment on Christmas Day in the form of a mock visit from an Admiral to convey Christmas greetings to the station's senior officers in 1918.

Wilfred Claude ROWLAND, hydrogen worker, was born in Reading on 11 May 1894. He was called by his second name, Claude, from a fairly early age. His civilian occupation was as a motor mechanic and driver.

On 18 February 1916, he joined the RNAS and was posted to *President II*, the training establishment at Crystal Palace, as an air mechanic second class. He was promoted to acting air mechanic first class in April 1917 and transferred to HMS *Daedalus*, a hulk in the Medway used as the nominal depot ship for all RNAS personnel serving on other stations, on 1 July 1917. His trade classification was hydrogen worker and he appears to have spent the rest of the war at Kingsnorth.

He was promoted to leading mechanic on 1 February 1918, which changed to corporal mechanic almost immediately when he transferred into the newly formed RAF. At this time he was earning 5s a day, over three times as much as a private, on one shilling and sixpence a day, which reflected the dangerous nature of hydrogen work. He passed his sergeant's exam on 29 October 1918. He moved to the discharge centre at Crystal Palace on 3 February 1919, was transferred to RAF G Reserve on 5 March 1919 and was 'deemed discharged' on 30 April 1920.

After the war he joined his father at Colebrook's (Reading) in the fishmonger and game department, married Margaret Ranson and had two sons. He died on 26 March 1937 of pulmonary tuberculosis aged 42, possibly as a result of the work with hydrogen that he was doing during the war.

E.R.A. SHAW was a crew member on the Parseval airship *P4*, who did in-flight repairs when the propeller blades broke. It was Shaw who recognised the fact that not only the broken blade but its opposite number would need to be replaced to ensure the engine was balanced.

William J. STANDFORD, a leading mechanic, was an early casualty. On Friday 23 April 1915 he was part of the ground crew trying to tether a newly arrived balloon. The wind was proving too strong and the crew couldn't hold it, so were forced to let go. William was either too slow or didn't hear the order to release the rope and was dragged up into the air. By the time he realised what had happened he was too high to safely let go. He hung on to the tethering rope as the ship rolled in the high winds. The crew in the airship vented gas to try to get the airship down quickly but eventually, having hung on for nearly ten minutes, his grip gave way and he fell about 500ft to his death (as mentioned earlier on p. 63).

Richard SWALLOW arrived at Kingsnorth in the early days of the station. Dick, as he was known, was a coxswain and was attached to the Kingsnorth erection party on North Sea-class airships. Here he gained a wealth of experience in airship construction and rigging. On 5 June 1917 he was gazetted probationary flight officer. He was transferred to Polegate and met with a fatal accident at the turn of the year. He was 26 years old.

Harry A. TANNER was one of the two art editors for *Flighty* in May 1917. He also employed his artistic skills for the benefit of the station concert party, painting their scenery and backdrops.

W.H. TAYLOR was a member of the Kingsnorth concert party in 1917.

H.W. TEMPLE was an air mechanic at Kingsnorth in 1917 and provided a serialised story for *Flighty* titled 'Poisoned Wells'. Later that year he was transferred to Malta, where he intended starting a similar magazine.

S. UPHAM was clearly a popular and rumbustious character. His messmates were quite happy to tease him in print, describing him as 'quiet' and 'meek' which he clearly was not. So, it is not surprising that he was also a member of the Kingsnorth concert party.

Arthur WALTERS worked in the Kingsnorth armoury. He left Kingsnorth to train as a seaplane pilot at Vendôme in France having been given a commissioned rank of second lieutenant.

Henry Richard WARD was born on 2 March 1899, the son of Percy Richard and Ellen Ward of High Street, Rolvenden, Kent. Harry was educated at Ashford Grammar School from 2 May 1913 to sometime in 1915. His name appears in the school's book of remembrance. He was an air mechanic second class (wireless telegraph operator) stationed at Kingsnorth before transferring to Howden. He was 18 when he was killed on Saturday 21 July 1917 in an accident when the *C11* airship burst into flames over the Humber, with the loss of two officers and two coxswains. He was returned home for burial locally in St Mary's Churchyard, Ashford, Kent.

A.E. WENN, was the honorary auditor for *Flighty* in July 1918.

Emma WORDEN joined the Wrens on 27 May 1918. She is listed in the National Archives with a rating of steward. The photograph was taken at about this time.

She served at Kingsnorth, later marrying Owen Way towards the end of 1928 in Hammersmith. They had three daughters.

CIVILIAN WORKERS

The airship factory and laboratories at Kingsnorth employed a large number of civilians, many of them drawn from the surrounding area. As well as the women employed in the fabric shops making hydrogen-proof balloon envelopes, both men and women worked on finishing the wooden airship cars, installing the engines and assembling the component parts to produce the completed airships. Only a few of these workers' names are known to us, but without their contribution Kingsnorth could not have produced the large number of airships needed to keep the shipping lanes safe from enemy submarines. They are listed in alphabetical order.

Neil Kensington ADAM was born on 5 November 1891, in Cambridge, the son of Dr James Adam, a Classics don from Aberdeen and senior tutor at Emmanuel College, Cambridge. He grew up in an academic atmosphere, surrounded by some of brightest academics in the country, so it is not surprising he did well at school. Neil specialised in physics, chemistry and maths at Winchester College and then studied Chemistry at Trinity College, Cambridge, where he became a fellow of the college. His contemporaries remembered him as 'a spare, ginger-haired young man of average height', who 'was always more interested in the comfort of his clothing than in looking elegant'.

In September 1914, aged 23, Neil's academic studies were interrupted by the war and he went to work as a chemist at the RNAS. Starting work at Farnborough, he transferred to Kingsnorth in 1915. His main challenge was to improve the rubber-proofed fabric used in the balloons of non-rigid airships; the need was for a light non-permeable fabric to retain hydrogen at pressure, a problem few manufacturers in this country had come close to solving at this time. Neil was also given a variety of other problems to solve while at Kingsnorth.

Neil's work at Kingsnorth brought him into contact with Winifred Wright, a mathematician working in the drawing office, and they married at Saint James' Church, Paddington, on 24 June 1916. Just over six months later, Neil received news that his only brother had been killed in France. He was devastated by the news and became very ill. The doctors diagnosed extreme nervous exhaustion and Winifred took him back to Cambridgeshire to recuperate. While ill, Neil became interested in the Christian Science Church, which he joined in the late summer of 1918. After his conversion to the Christian Science movement, he began to recover and he returned to his studies at Cambridge University.

After the war Neil spent two years studying biochemistry. He then moved from biochemistry to the study of mono-molecular surface films on water and in 1921 he was appointed Royal Society Research fellow at the University of Sheffield. After working in Sheffield for eight years, Neil lectured in Physical Chemistry at University College London and was elected a member of the Royal Society while he was there. In 1937 he moved to become head of the Chemistry Department at the University of Southampton. In 1939 Neil watched another generation of students march off to war. The technology of aerial warfare had developed in leaps and bounds since his work at Kingsnorth. In 1957 Neil retired from the university.

He died at his home in Southampton on 19 July 1973, aged 82. Peter Morris, in a biographical article, concluded: 'Prof. Adam was noted for his clear, incisive and economical written style which cut through academic vagueness, incoherence and gobbledegook. His ability to write in unambiguous terms ensured the usefulness of his papers and the textbooks he wrote.' Winifred died the following month (see also pp. 155–6).

Alfred BATES, from Farningham (about 12 miles away from Kingsnorth as the crow flies), was ground crew, working as a driver. Many of the staff at the station were relatively local and returned home once the war was over. Alf, as he was known, was one of the people who acquired a copy of a photograph taken in 1919 which was taken of the air station staff, both military and civilian. His daughter Jean Cload, kept this photo rolled up in a plastic carrier bag in a cupboard until 2009, when she saw a television appeal for information and contacted the BBC. The Fleet Air Arm arranged a plaque at Kingsnorth Power Station to commemorate the airship station and copied the photo for their archives before returning it to Jean, beautifully framed.

Arthur Robert GRIGGS was born in the autumn of 1888 and grew up in Bromley, where he worked as a gas engineer's assistant and draughtsman.

Griggs was appointed as chief chemist at the hydrogen laboratory at Kingsnorth in December 1916. For the next two years he was employed in the production of hydrogen using the water-gas process, during which time he met Germaine Marie Eugenie Paule Amigues, a 25-year-old French woman who was probably taking refuge from the horrors of war on the continent. They were married in the summer of 1917 in Wandsworth. In 1918 Griggs contributed to part two of the *Hydrogen Manual* compiled by Lieutenant Colonel T.A. Monkton. He received compensation for disability in 1919 after doctors warned him that he would need some time to recuperate from the effects of gas inhalation and he would be unable to work with hydrogen without the symptoms recurring.

Despite this, after the war he continued working on hydrogen-production methods. On 20 December 1921 he filed a patent in Canada titled 'Production of Hydrogen', and on 28 August 1923 he filed one in the USA titled 'Hydrogen Production'. Arthur and Germaine lived for a few years in Kensington before moving to Leatherhead. In December 1927, the couple travelled from Cherbourg to New York, returning in July 1928.

He died on 14 July 1943, aged 55. Germaine moved to Cornwall and died there in 1960.

May HOOKER was employed in the inspection and marking-out department from 1 January 1916 until April 1919. On 24 April 1920, Mr McWade supplied Miss Hooker with a letter of recommendation to aid her search for employment. In it he describes her as, 'Energetic, Painstaking, and an excellent timekeeper'. In 1917 her parents, who lived at 22 Clarence Place, Gravesend, came to visit her at Kingsnorth.

Florence Elizabeth MISKIN was the daughter of a labourer working as a plate-layer on the government railway. She was born on 6 September 1891, and in 1911, 19-year-old Florrie was working, like her older sister Matilda, as a housemaid. If they were related to the Miskins living at Beluncle, it was a distant enough connection that they do not appear to have benefited from the relationship.

Florrie was interviewed by Phillip MacDougall for his article 'From Airship Station to Oil Refinery'. She was one of the large number of young girls employed in the fabric shop and remembered that one of her duties had been helping weigh down landing airships, for which task she had to wear a special pair of heavy boots. Even with the boots this was a dangerous job. She was also a member of the ladies' tug-of-war team.

After the war, in the autumn of 1921, Florrie married Ernest W. Day and their son John was born the following year. Florrie died in 1985 aged 93.

Andy MUIR, in addition to his station duties, was the advertisement manager for *Flighty* in July 1918.

Jessie PELLING was one of the civilian staff who kept a copy of the panoramic staff photograph. Her son Jack, in an interview with the local newspaper, said that his mother, who was about 30 when the war started, was a gas welder on the aluminium-framed airships and that her job was to weld the mighty sections into place. There were no men to do the job because by this time most men had been drafted into the trenches in France.

The non-rigid airships built at Kingsnorth did not have a metal framework, unlike the rigid airships, and steel was kept to a minimum to reduce weight, so only a very little welding was needed on the framework of the gondolas. Aluminium is light, so was used to clad the gondola frames of the larger airships. If she was working on the gondolas or cars for the Coastal or North Sea airships, she probably worked with both metals, the welding being what she remembered most clearly.

Jessie lived in the Medway area until her death aged 88.

Elsie Eleanor PERKINS was a farm horseman's daughter born on 17 September 1900. When the First World War started, Elsie was living in Wainscott, about 5 miles west of Kingsnorth. She told her niece that during the war she worked as a French polisher on the airships, polishing the wooden instrument panels. It made her niece think of the labour (and beauty) that had gone into these machines.

Elsie married Albert Cecil James Eldridge in the autumn of 1926 and they had one child, Cecil, the following year, but he died soon after he was born. Widowed during the summer of 1976, Elsie lived all her life in the Medway area and reached the ripe old age of 97 before she died in 1998.

PLAYER, in addition to his official duties, organised religious meetings in Kingsnorth's YMCA hut.

John William POOLEY was born in 1897. The son of a watchmaker, he was educated at Reigate Grammar School and King's College London. He became assistant chemist at Kingsnorth Airship Station.

In March 1919, he became an associate of the Royal Society under the special provisions of the regulations adopted by the council in July 1917 and 1918. At this time he was still living in civilians' quarters at Kingsnorth. After a few months with Alexander Duckham & Co., he joined the staff of a government laboratory.

He never married. At the time of his death he was based in Lancashire, one of the senior chemists and in charge of the *Ad Valorem* duties section. He died at the age of 51 on 20 July 1948.

Arthur David RITCHIE, born in Oxford on 22 June 1891, moved to Edinburgh with his family and went to the University of St Andrews, where he graduated with first-class honours in 1911. He then went on to Trinity College, Cambridge, until the First World War interrupted his education.

He joined the RNAS and was chief chemist at Kingsnorth in April 1918, where he wrote, amongst other things, an extensive report on the permeability and endurance of rubbered fabrics. His broad approach to science enabled him to take on new ideas and be open to suggestions.

After the war he returned to Cambridge, where he wrote his dissertation on scientific method. Soon after he was appointed as a lecturer in biological chemistry in 1922 and two years later in physiological chemistry at the University of Manchester. He continued at Manchester, holding the Sir Samuel Hall Chair of Philosophy from 1937 to 1945. At this time he moved to the University of Edinburgh, where he held the Chair of Logic and Metaphysics until his retirement in 1959.

Dr Ritchie died in 1967.

George Gustavious Frederick William SELLICK was born around January 1882 in Heavitree, near Honiton, Devon. By 1911 he had shortened his name and appears on the census as Frederick, a cabinet-maker in Exeter employing two men. He may have been working on such things as instrument panels, which would link in with the memory of Elsie Perkins above.

He and his wife Alice had four children when she filed for divorce in 1925. He married May Ellis the following year and they had another two sons. He died on 15 January 1950 in Newton Abbot, Devon.

Eric SMITH was employed in the experimental laboratories, where they were developing lighter alloys, probably for airship cables. This was his first job on leaving school and he was paid sixteen shillings a week, a very good wage for a first job when the average wage was about £1 a week.

Ada M. STRATFORD worked in the Kingsnorth fabric shop before her marriage to Nelson Clifton on New Year's Day 1918 at Hoo.

TODD became involved in the life of the station, as well as carrying out his official work, and was instrumental in setting up the Kingsnorth Concert Party in November 1916.

Amy R. WATSON was one of the two women chemists employed in the chemical laboratory at Kingsnorth out of a total staff of seven. She started in August 1916 and moved on to work at Cardington in February 1921. The work required a good general knowledge of chemistry to university-degree standard.

Much work was done on the rubber-coated fabric used to make the gas-proof envelopes, the object being to produce a low-weight fabric of high tensile strength and low permeability. The next most frequent work involved tests on the quality of the hydrogen gas at output and when it had been in the balloons for some time. She was also involved in testing the materials used in hydrogen production both for the silicol method and, in the later stages of the war, the iron ore used in the water-gas process.

Marjorie Gwynne WRIGHT was born around 1892. She was one of the four women employed in the engineers' drawing office at Kingsnorth, possibly recruited by her cousin Winifred who also worked there. She married Wing Commander Cave-Brown-Cave on 8 June 1918 at Holy Trinity Parish Church, Clapham. They had three children, John, Gillian and Thomas.

She died on 8 November 1969, the same year as her husband (see p. 107).

Winifred WRIGHT was born on 11 April 1886 in Wyke, Yorkshire. Winifred was the daughter of a solicitor and was educated at a boarding school in Harrogate.

While working in the engineers' drawing office at Kingsnorth, Winifred met Neil Adam (see above), a senior chemist in the neighbouring laboratories, and married him on 24 June 1916, at the parish church of Saint James, Paddington. After her marriage, Winifred left the drawing office and about six months later nursed her husband when he collapsed with 'nervous exhaustion'. It was at this time that they became Christian Scientists.

After the war, Winifred was living at End House, Owlstone Roadd, Cambridge, where she was contacted in 1921 by a Miss Conway, who was collecting information on the work of women during the war. Winifred wrote a detailed description of what her work had entailed: doing complex calculations to produce data for the designers. The work required intelligence and practical mathematical and scientific knowledge. Slide rules were used to obtain results quickly and accurately.

She died in Southampton a month after her husband, in August 1973.

APPENDIX

AIRSHIP STATION TIMELINE

Late summer 1912	Kingsnorth Farm identified as suitable site for airship station.
October 1912	Chatham's Director of Works marked out site for airship shed.
December 1912	Negotiations started to buy additional adjacent land.
April 1913	Work began on preparing the ground for the airship sheds.
May 1913	Work began on erecting metal airship shed.
July 1913	Vickers given contract for wooden airship shed.
February 1914	Winston Churchill, First Lord of the Admiralty, visits.
April 1914	Neville Florian Usborne appointed station commander.
May 1914	Airship staff started to arrive.
June 1914	Serious fire in metal airship shed.
June 1914	RNAS formed.
August 1914	War declared.
August 1914	Lieutenant LeFroy arrived with wireless equipment for airships and first patrol carried out.
September 1914	Land purchase completed.

October 1914	Oil-storage and electricity- and hydrogen-generation facilities underway.
November 1914	HMS *Bulwark* exploded.
December 1914	Gale-force winds caused considerable damage to buildings.
March 1915	Design staff and equipment arrived from Farnborough.
March 1915	*SS1* designed, produced, trialled and put into service.
Spring 1915	Pilot training commenced.
May 1915	First Coastal-class airship trial flight.
February 1916	Commanders Usborne and Ireland killed in *AP1* crash.
December 1916	Pilot training moved to Cranwell.
December 1916	Arthur R. Griggs appointed as chief chemist.
January 1917	Water-gas hydrogen plant opens.
February 1917	First North Sea-class airship trial flight.
April 1917	Station magazine *Flighty* started.
November 1918	Preparations for new electrolytic gas plant underway.
November 1918	Armistice signed.
November 1918	Non-rigid airship construction abandoned.
1919	Proposed to use station for kite-balloon experiments.
January 1919	Old Boys' Association formed.
February 1922	Site advertised for sale.
1935	Commemorative edition of *Flighty* published.

SOURCES

PRIMARY

The National Archives

Census returns, 1851–1911

ADM 1/8524/128 Airship stations at Kingsnorth, Wormwood Scrubs and White City

ADM 116/1305 Kingsnorth – Chatham – Acquisition of land for aviation, etc.

ADM 178/37 Commander Murray F. Sueter's papers

ADM 188/1026 Royal Navy records of seamen's services

ADM 273 Admiralty Officers' records

AIR 1/146/15/62 Defence of Kingsnorth … against enemy raids and landings – orders for …

AIR 1/188 Dover, Skegness … Kingsnorth – daily reports of operations Aug–Dec 1914

AIR 1/354/15/227/10 Inspecting Captain of Aircraft, Sheerness Office, correspondence and papers relating to Kingsnorth …

AIR 1/355/15/227/11 Inspecting Captain of Aircraft, Sheerness Office, correspondence and papers relating to Felixstowe … and Kingsnorth …

AIR 1/408/15/236/2 RNAS provision of … and additional buildings at Kingsnorth

AIR 1/645/17/122/329 Allocation of three SS airships for patrol work at Kingsnorth …

AIR 1/2453 List of officers lent to RNAS

AIR 1/2512 3 & 4 Disposition of RNAS officers

AIR 1/2630 Photographs of Commander Usborne

AIR 1/2656 Use of asphyxiating gases

AIR 1/2657 Maps showing sitings for aircraft bases

AIR 2/15 Report by Chief Chemist, Airship Construction Station, Kingsnorth …

AIR 2/37 Kingsnorth Station Experimental Bulletin for Sep 1917

AIR 2/40 Kingsnorth: non-metallic petrol tank. Report on experiments
1917

AIR 2/52 Kingsnorth: petrol tanks 1917–18

AIR 2/132 Provision of accommodation at Kingsnorth for kite balloon
work

AVIA 20/565 Elastic cord from Kingsnorth: tests

DSIR 23/806 Visit to the RN Airship Station, Kingsnorth 1916

DSIR 23/9814 Kingsnorth chemical laboratory: work planned or in progress

IR 95/61/151 Kingsnorth

MT 58/476 Kingsnorth Light Railway, 1926

T 1/11651 Admiralty: establishment of a naval air station at Kingsnorth Farm
on the Medway: compensation to lessee for immediate surrender of his
lease; purchase of additional land

T 1/12353 Admiralty: A.R. Griggs, Chief Chemist, Hydrogen Laboratory,
Kingsnorth, [Kent]: compensation for disability

Imperial War Museum

J.S. Middleton, interview. Imperial War Museum sound archive, catalogue no.
38, reel 4

Victor Goddard, interview. Imperial War Museum sound archive, catalogue
no. 303, reel 16

Thomas Blenheim Williams, interview. Imperial War Museum sound archive,
catalogue no. 313, reels 3 & 12

MUN 15 2/2, 3, 6, 7, 8. Correspondence and reports re work in engineers'
drawing office at Kingsnorth Airship Station

MUN 14 2/4,5 Correspondence and report re work done by women in the
chemical laboratory of Kingsnorth Airship Station

RAF Museum archive

The Innocent Erk by Gilbert Holland Price. Unpublished manuscript written
c. 1920

Flighty. Kingsnorth Airship Station's magazine published monthly, May 1917–
January 1918, & 1935 Reunion souvenir edition

Fleet Air Arm Museum archive
Photographs and plans

Flight Global Archive
Flight Magazine contains numerous articles relating to Kingsnorth and its
officers

Medway Archives
Chatham News, various issues
Maps and photographs
The Navy List, published monthly lists of information on ships, stations and
 serving officers

The London Gazette Archive
Information on serving officers promotions and decorations

Museum of English Rural Life Archive
TR MES AD1/1051 1915. Works correspondence regarding the building of a
 hut and a garage

Other
Hydrogen Manual, published by the Royal Naval Air Service, 1916, describes
 hydrogen production by the silicol method
Hydrogen Manual, published by the Royal Air Force, 1920, contains
 information on both methods of hydrogen production
Northern Territory Times and Gazette, Saturday 21 June 1919, contains an article
 on using airships for minesweeping
Kelly's Directories for Kent
Williams, T.B. *Airship Pilot No. 28.* (London: William Kimber, 1974)

SECONDARY

Articles and Reports
'Lodge Hill and Upnor Railway', by D. Yeatman. *The Industrial Railway
 Record*, no. 12, pp. 277–92
'Neil Kensington Adam, obituary'. *Biographical Memoirs of Fellows of the Royal
 Society*, vol. 20, pp. 1–26
'When Airships Flew at Capel', by David G. Collier. *Kent Life*, June 1975, p. 4
'Hamilton Hartridge, obituary'. *British Medical Journal*, 20 March 1976, p. 716
'Hamilton Hartridge, obituary'. *Biographical Memoirs of Fellows of the Royal
 Society*, vol. 23, pp. 193–211
'A History of Kingsnorth Airship Station', by John Davis. *The journal of the
 Association of World War One Aero-Historians*, 1989
'The Accidental Death of HMS *Bulwark* (1914)', by Richard Stackpoole-
 Ryding. *Medal News*, September 1991
'Loss of *NS11* – A Local View', by Nick Walmsley. *Dirigible* (the journal of the
 Airship Heritage Trust), summer 1994
Various articles from *Cross & Cockade*

'From Airship Station to Oil Refinery', by Philip MacDougall, *Coast & Country*, Vol. 8, No. 3, p. 14

'Hydrogen for Airships', by A.M. Burgess. *Cleveland Industrial Archaeology Society Newsletter*, 82

'Kingsnorth Power Station, Isle of Grain – excavation report', by Neil Griffin. *Archaeology South-East*, 2006

'VIP Jean has special day at power station', by Keyan Milanian. *Medway Messenger*, 5 February 2009

Damhead Creek 2 Archaeological Background, by Parsons Brinckerhoff Ltd. PB Power for Scottish Power Ltd, June 2009

Books

Ashworth, C., *Action Stations – Military Airfields of the Central South and South-east.* 2nd ed. (Yeovil: Patrick Stephens, 1990)

Brabner, J.H.F., *The Comprehensive Gazetteer of England and Wales* (London: William Mackenzie, 1894)

Castle, I., *British Airships 1905–1930* (Oxford: Osprey Books, 2009)

Corser, W.J.L., *Wings on Rails: Industrial Railways in the Logistic Support of Britain's Air Defence Forces 1914–1994* (London: Arcturus Press, 2003)

Countryman, B., *The R101: Her Voyage to Canada* (Erin, Ontario: Boston Mills Press, 1982)

Francis, P., *British Military Airfield Architecture – From Airships to the Jet Age* (Yeovil: Patrick Stephens, 1966)

Gladwell, A., *River Medway Pleasure Steamers* (Stroud, UK: Amberley Publishing, 2010)

Hasted, E., *History and Topographical Survey of the County of Kent.* Vol. 4 (Canterbury: W. Bristow, 1798)

Mowthorpe, C., *Battle Bags, British Airships of the First World War* (Stroud, UK: Sutton Publishing, 1995)

Plummer, S.J., *A Man of Invention* (Raleigh, NC: Lulu, 2010)

Raleigh, W., *The War in the Air* (Oxford: Clarendon Press, 1922)

Sinclair, J.A., *Airships in Peace and War* (London: Rich & Cowan, 1934)

Slater, G., *The English Peasantry and the Enclosure of Common* (Hong Kong: Forgotten Books, 2012 [1907])

Ventry, A.F.D.E.-de M. (Lord), and E.M. Kolesnik., *Airship Saga: The History of Airships Seen Through the Eyes of the Men who Designed, Built and Flew Them* (London: Cassell Illustrated, 1982)

Warner, G., *Airships over the North Channel* (Newtownards, NI: April Sky Design, 2005)

Whale, G., *British Airships: Past, Present and Future* (London: John Lane, The Bodley Head, 1919)

Worsdale, D., *Hoo St Werburgh in Old Picture Postcards* (Someren-Eind, NL: Europese Bibliotheek, 1984)

Worsdale, D., *Hoo Hundred in Old Picture Postcards* (Someren-Eind, NL: Europese Bibliotheek, 1989)

Forums

http://www.kenthistoryforum.co.uk/index.php?topic=9871.0

http://1914-1918.invisionzone.com/forums/index.php?showtopic=74409

http://www.airfieldinformationexchange.org/community/showthread.php?9581-Kingsnorth

http://www.theaerodrome.com/forum/people/37729-kingsnorth-airship-hanger.html

http://www.worldnavalships.com/forums/showthread.php?t=10210

Websites

These website links were active at the time of going to press, but you should be aware that links often change or disappear.

Hoo St Werburg by Arthur Vidgeon. http://www.whitehousefarm.eclipse.co.uk/oldhoo/hoointro.htm

Archaeology South-East. http://archaeologyse.co.uk/04-Projects/Kent/Kingsnorth/index.htm

The Airship Heritage Trust. http://www.airshipsonline.com/airships/imperial/Airship%20Station.htm

Flight Global Archive. http://www.flightglobal.com/pdfarchive/index.html

Fleet Air Arm Officers' Association. http://www.fleetairarmoa.org/pages/fleet_air_arm_history/history.shtml

RAF Museum. http://www.rafmuseum.org.uk/milestones-of-flight/british_military/1914.cfm

Medway Campus. http://campus.medway.ac.uk/library/about/files/daybyday/march.pdf

Kingsnorth Light Railway. http://www.britishrailways.info/INDEPENDENT%20LINES%20A-L.htm

British Listed Buildings. http://www.britishlistedbuildings.co.uk/en-505260-former-airship-shed-at-moat-farm-st-mary

Airship Heritage Trust. http://www.aht.ndirect.co.uk/airships/ss/index.html

Details of the flight of SR1 from Italy to England. http://www.rogersstudy.co.uk/misc/sr1/sr1.html

Naval History, 1915. http://www.naval-history.net/WW1NavyBritishLGDecorations1915.htm

Neville Usborne family-tree website. http://www.usbornefamilytree.com/
    neville1883.htm
Dambusters website. http://www.dambusters.biz/war-personalities/leaders/
    sir-ralph-cochrane/
Information regarding Francis Robert Edward Davis. http://
    ourheritagewarmedals.co.uk/id22.htm
Report on military aviation at night. http://www.dtic.mil/cgi-bin/GetTR
    Doc?AD=ADA243350&Location=U2&doc=GetTRDoc.pdf
Naval Historical Collectors and Research Association website. http://nhcra-
    online.org/20c/robins.html

INDEX

If you enjoyed this book, you may also be interested in…

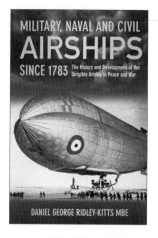

Military, Naval and Civil Airships Since 1783
DANIEL GEORGE RIDLEY-KITTS

This book traces the development of the airship, relating the struggles of the early pioneers, from the Montgolfier brothers, and the parallel of the hydrogen balloon. Between the wars it appeared that the giant passenger-carrying airships offered the solution to long-distance air travel, but this dream proved illusory. In the present age, airships are again being considered for new uses, including airborne military command posts and geostationary unmanned 'Aerostats' harvesting the power of the Jetsream to provide an umlimited supply of electrical power for the planet.

978 0 7524 6471 8

R101: A Pictorial History
NICK LE NEVE WALMSLEY

At the time of her construction in the late 1920s, His Majesty's Airship *R101* was the largest flying object ever made. As Britain recovered from the First World War, *R101*'s graceful lines, vast size and luxurious accommodation came to represent the supreme self-confidence and hopes of a nation. But that unclouded vision was fatally coloured by personal ambition and political intrigue that touched many lives and reached a terrible climax on a storm-lashed hillside in France on 5 October 1930. *R101* has wide appeal to aviation enthusiasts, social historians and anyone fascinated by a tale of a heroic dream with a horrific end.

978 0 7524 5683 6

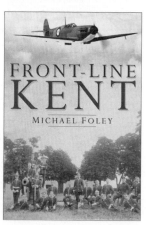

Front-Line Kent
MICHAEL FOLEY

In all major conflicts, many people in Kent have lived closer to the enemy in Europe than to London. Much of the county's coastline has been the site of training and weapon development, which adds to the interest of military sites in this area. Michael Foley's book delves into the long history of military Kent, from Roman forts to Martello towers, built to keep Napoleon out, from the ambitious Royal Military Canal, which cost an equivalent of GBP 10 million in today's money but was abandoned after seventy years, to wartime airfields and underground Cold War installations. This lively and informative book will appeal to anyone interested in Kent's history.

978 0 7509 4460 1